Poetry Ireland Review 121

Eagarthóir / Editor
EAVAN BOLAND

© Poetry Ireland Ltd 2017

Poetry Ireland Ltd/Éigse Éireann Teo gratefully acknowledges the assistance of The Arts Council/An Chomhairle Ealaíon and The Arts Council of Northern Ireland.

Poetry Ireland invites individuals and commercial organizations to become Friends of Poetry Ireland. For more details, please contact:

Poetry Ireland Friends Scheme, Poetry Ireland, 11 Parnell Square East, Dublin 1, Ireland

or telephone +353 1 6789815; e-mail info@poetryireland.ie

FRIENDS:
Joan and Joe McBreen, Desmond Windle, Neville Keery,
Noel and Anne Monahan, Ruth Webster, Maurice Earls,
Mary Shine Thompson, Seán Coyle, Henry and Deirdre Comerford,
Thomas Dillon Redshaw, Rachel Joynt

Poetry Ireland Review is published three times a year by Poetry Ireland Ltd. The Editor enjoys complete autonomy in the choice of material published. The contents of this publication should not be taken to reflect either the views or the policy of the publishers.

ISBN: 1-902121-69-4
ISSN: 0332-2998

ASSISTANT EDITOR: **Paul Lenehan**, with the assistance of **Elizabeth McIntosh, Erin Anderson, Orla Higgins,** and **Natalie Lewendon**

IRISH-LANGUAGE EDITOR: **Liam Carson**

DESIGN: **Alistair Keady** (www.hexhibit.com)

COVER CREDIT: from 'Parallelism' (screenprint, 77H x 58W CM) by **Neil Dunne**
See www.neildavidjames.com

Contents

Eavan Boland	5	EDITORIAL
Wendy Holborow	7	I SEE HER
Susannah Dickey	8	XENOMELIA
Kenneth Fields	10	CADUCITY
Liam Carson	11	REVIEW: LO KWA MEI-EN, ANNA JOURNEY
Thomas McCarthy	16	LAST SERVICE IN THE ORTHODOX SYNAGOGUE
Laura Webb	17	SUBJECTIVITY
John Kinsella	18	THE GALE LIFTS THE ROOF OFF THE 90,000 LITRE TANK
Kevin Cantwell	19	AN ESSAY ON TYPOGRAPHY
Eavan Boland	20	ESSAY: BRIGIT PEGEEN KELLY
Brigit Pegeen Kelly	26	SONG
Diarmuid Johnson	28	NÍ FUATH LINN
	29	NEAD DREOILÍN
	30	NÍ FÉIDIR COILL A CHUR
Michael Hofmann	31	REVIEW: PAUL MULDOON
Leontia Flynn	34	28
Jean O'Brien	35	THE MOST EXPENSIVE HEN HOUSE IN ENGLAND
Matthew Sweeney	37	TIN MINING
Katie Donovan	38	REVIEW: JAMIE MCKENDRICK, VONA GROARKE
Eavan Boland	42	FEATURED POET: SOLMAZ SHARIF
Solmaz Sharif	44	LOOK
	46	MASTER FILM
Colm Tóibín	47	ESSAY: PAULA MEEHAN
Andrew Jamison	52	ANTI-ACKNOWLEDGEMENTS
Anne Maher	54	DOWN MEMORY LANE
A.M. Cousins	55	BEDSIT
Proinsias Ó Drisceoil	56	REVIEW: JOHN MCDONALD, GABRIEL ROSENSTOCK, AILBHE NÍ GHEARBHUIGH
Paul Perry	62	THE END OF SUMMER
John W Sexton	65	ONE COGNIZANCE
Colette Colfer	66	MINOTAUR
Michael O'Loughlin	67	INTERVIEW: YVES BONNEFOY
Jean Bleakney	75	STALWART
Chelsea Whitton	76	GRASSHOPPERS
Gerard Smyth	78	THE HORSE CAME BACK BUT NOT THE RIDER
Theo Dorgan	79	ESSAY: JOHN MONTAGUE: THE INFLUENCE OF ANXIETY
	85	GOING HOME
Aifric Mac Aodha	86	GÓ
	87	LIED
Richard W Halperin	94	BY A FIRESIDE, DECEMBER

Thomas Dillon Redshaw	95	REVIEW: THOMAS MCCARTHY, MARY O'MALLEY
Eithne Hand	99	HARD CHAW
Iggy McGovern	100	HYPERMETROPIA
Emily Holt	101	OUR RED EVENING
Dáibhidh Thomáis Albanach	102	REVIEW: SÉAMUS BARRA Ó SÚILLEABHÁIN, SIMON Ó FAOLÁIN, DIARMUID JOHNSON
Jane Clarke	106	HE STOOD AT THE TOP OF THE STAIRS
Tom French	107	BANK
Stephen Sexton	108	THE CURFEW
Ron Houchin	110	ROY ORBISON'S GLASSES
Joseph Woods	111	LET US FLY AWAY TO THE FAMED CITIES OF ASIA
Martin Malone	115	REVIEW: SIMON ARMITAGE, PETER SIRR
Shirley Gorby	119	VISITING THE SEAMSTRESS
Conor Cleary	120	WEBBING
Majella Kelly	121	MICHAELMAS DAISIES

Notes on Contributors 122

Editorial

A CONVERSATION

I'm honoured to be editing *Poetry Ireland Review*, and particularly pleased to be following Vona Groarke's fine editorship. Taking on my own, I have had very strong support. So before I go further I want to thank Paul Lenehan and Maureen Kennelly for their generous help with this issue.

An editorship is a vantage point. Even so, it's never easy to have an overview of what's happening in poetry. So much changes, and so quickly. In addition to that, poetry can struggle in both a social and private context, and fashion and neglect all too often overlay both.

But looked at closely, something does emerge: a conversation. Noisy and fractious certainly, and given to monologue at times rather than dialogue. But a conversation nevertheless that can be thrilling in its reach and commitment. And that's what I've wanted to suggest here, however briefly: A conversation made up of poems, of course, but also of the energies that swirl around them – the ideas, the debates, the disagreements.

Since I divide the year between Ireland and the USA, I meet with poetry in both places. Different histories, different traditions. I also keep bumping into the realization that the world is contracting. Technology and travel allow me – as it does so many other people – to be a reader and writer in both places. Editing this issue gives me a chance to bring some American voices with me, while pointing, as *PIR* always has, to the vitality of Irish poetry.

The poetic conversation is a fixture: it doesn't change to comply with change. Technology has not, I believe, shaped it so much as revealed it. It's easier now to see links between the excerpt in this issue from Yves Bonnefoy's interview – reprinted here from decades ago – with his reverence for Yeats's 'admirable poems of time passing', and Theo Dorgan's sense of learning 'craft, duty, fidelity to the self-intending poem' from John Montague. Kenneth Fields's fine poem on age gestures towards themes of Yeats. 'Look', one of two featured poems by the remarkable young American poet Solmaz Sharif, is charged with a menace and self-awareness Yves Bonnefoy would have recognized.

Inevitably, this is also a conversation of contrasts. Paula Meehan's lectures, given as the Ireland Professor of Poetry – perceptively assessed here by Colm Tóibín – commend a generous life for the working poet: an outreach to the earth, to the planet, an insistence on our imaginative obligations to both. But the remarkable American poet who died recently, Brigit Pegeen Kelly, who I write about in this issue, made no obviously purposeful statements. Her exemplary poems tend to the hermetic, the pure and inward reflection. Yet there can be no doubt that both poets, Meehan and Kelly, from different viewpoints, add texture and depth to the conversation.

The most exciting part of this editorship has been reading the submitted poems. Going through them – poem after poem, image after image – brought back a cherished memory. Standing in a bookstore in Dublin when I was a young poet – Greene's in Clare St, or Hodges Figgis perhaps – taking a journal down from the shelf and opening it at a new poem. And, if I was lucky, feeling there and then the intense lifelong companionship of good poetry. The poems I chose for this issue shook out that memory. Except this time they were in the present not the past. There are poems here from several countries, written under various skies. But the Irish work was a special revelation of the un-derivative vitality of poems on this island.

Even if the continuance of a poetic conversation – given the constraints of space – can only be hinted at here, its reach into the lives and work of poets and readers makes it a permanent resource. And yet, in our time, often a fragile one. It always needs the protection of its stake-holders. Since I was a young poet, right up to the present, Poetry Ireland has been a mainstay for poets and readers – all the way from workshops to events to publications. Never failing to remind a community of the importance of this art. Generating at every stage new parts of this conversation. And never failing to protect it.

Eavan Boland

Wendy Holborow

I SEE HER

I see her through a cubist's eye
chiselled planes & angles mingle in black & white
disentangled, broken up & rearranged
in geometric form.

I see her through an impressionist's eye
rapid dabs of paint, dots, distorted,
sparkling patches of light & colour –
incandescent.

I see her through a miniaturist's eye
minute, modelled like a doll held in the palm
of a hand, such infinite patience,
dexterous.

I see her through a surrealist's eye
confusion, un-recognisable in shape or form,
her reality disguised in the triptych mirror of art –
instinctive.

I see her through an icon painter's eye
dark image illumed by silver & gold, a halo
above her head, so exquisite it is considered
acheiropoieta.

I see her through a portrait painter's eye
perfect in every detail as she gazes
out of the canvas of imperfection, her inner essence,
unveiled,

a slight smile, gentle contentment,
no smudges of a dark fanciful world apparent in
her reasoned demeanour as she sits,
poses.

Susannah Dickey

XENOMELIA

I visit the home of a man who is recently deceased.
He opens the door and I go to take off my shoes –
he says, "Don't worry, that kind of thing doesn't bother
me anymore."
When he takes my hand I feel aware of my skin
as being like flabby batter on my skeleton.
It feels loose,
a dusty garment hanging in the costume department
of an abandoned theatre.
I tell him my teeth have been feeling wrong in my head
lately. I've had thoughts of breaking them with
hammers, putting my fingers to my gums and feeling them
come away in brown threads
like the flesh of overripe bananas. I ask
if he thinks I might be suffering
from some syndrome and he says,
"I once attended a medical conference. A drug rep
told a joke with the punch line: 'Of course not! He's dyslexic!'
and the premise seemed to be that it is inconceivable to think
the children of doctors might just be stupid."
I say, "Isn't that horribly insensitive?"
and he says, "Probably,
but then, that kind of thing doesn't bother
me anymore."
Outside, the rain has hardened to hail and the high-pitched
hollow *taptaptap* of gristle on the window makes me
feel like a lobster in the tank
of a mid-priced restaurant.
We sit in the dark on sofas coated in brown velour
– the sort worn in cop shows set in the '70s.
On a greasy glass table is a bowl filled with
translucent, unwrapped sweets. I lift one, then put it back.
We watch the snooker and he tries to explain the rules.
I make a bad joke about sinking the pink and
I understand why he no longer feels obliged
to smile politely.
The sex is rhythmic and solipsistic:
I'm thinking about making myself
an appointment at the dentist and he doesn't so much

come as his whole body wilts in my arms
like a sleeping bag.
I put my fingers to my thighs and find a light coating
of what feels like icing sugar.
When I go to the door I say, "I forgot to ask you how you died'
and he says, 'That kind of thing doesn't bother
me anymore."
The hail has stopped and I look for my shoes.
He reminds me that I'm still wearing them.

Kenneth Fields

CADUCITY

Across the quad I see them coming, pairs,
Singles, groups, old men
Leaving a memorial service for a teacher
    Older than me.

Some are with canes, some walkers. Wispy white
Hair thins in a breeze that blows one
Off his stride, a feather. Overhead
    The air rumbles,

Machines designed, like everything, to drop –
The compassionate heart encased
In carbon fibre, wired
    For complete destruction.

The ground trembles. These old men,
Veterans, some of them,
Of wars six worlds down, speak to each other,
    Grateful, as I am, for any day.

If I saluted, someone would return it. Today
We hold these arcades. Palms and bays
And loquats, wanderers out of China, shade us
    All equally.

Liam Carson

BODY OF WORK

Lo Kwa Mei-en, *Yearling* (Alice James Books, 2015), $15.95.
Anna Journey, *The Atheist Wore Goat Silk* (Louisiana State University Press, 2017), $19.95.

> I was desperately working to write myself back into ownership of my body. I was living with choices that other people had made about my body, and having much difficulty making choices that my body could survive. I was living with the simultaneous drives to self-preserve and self-destruct and poetry was the only creative force I believed in at the time. So the first conscious choice I made about the body in my poems was allowing it to exist within them at all.
> – LO KWA MEI-EN, INTERVIEW WITH GUERNICA, 02/02/2016

Like Walt Whitman, American poet Lo Kwa Mei-en sings 'the body electric'. The poems in her debut collection *Yearling* are visceral explorations of the connection between body and language, crackling with taut energies. If at first they appear opaque, they are anything but meaningless. She takes clichés and dead metaphors, deconstructs them and infuses them with startling new meanings. 'I mean what I slay', she declares in 'Era for Forgiveness'.

The body is the portal through which to enter Mei-en's highly symbolic lexicon. In 'Arrow', the body is 'a dictionary of only chances'. In 'The Body with an Elegy inside of it', she speaks of 'what made the missive figs grow / fat as a love word rounding a lip and finite / as the body addressed'. There's a terrific sense of pressure and release in 'Devil of Defiance' – 'the want of breakable / skin a sign of what breaks'; the sense of a dam-burst of language – the sun 'breaks / through a cloud's belly, radiant', while she hails 'every body / swollen as a sail' ('This is Siren Country'). In her opening poem 'Ariel' (with its conscious echoes both of Shakespeare's *Tempest* and Sylvia Plath's *Ariel*), Mei-en writes: 'The hour swelled, / glassy, splitting / like a lip'. The poet's consciousness also cries out to be *known* – 'know me harder' ('Era of Forgiveness').

The mouth and the throat create speech. In 'Yearling and Armor', the poet feels 'the body move again / like a mouthful of sea'. 'Devil of Defiance' carries an erotic charge ('undone like the mane of god and wanting for flood'; 'throw me down on bales of bold / earth'). The 'hot, cracking throat' of this poem becomes 'the summer / attic of the throat' in 'Becoming Radio'. In the very next poem, 'Rough Husbandry', there's 'I keep my hand on the throat of every small death'. Mei-en's poems segue into one another throughout *Yearling*; it's a beautifully constructed collection, a symphonic weave of imagistic threads. Again and again there are swallows, meteors, radios, stars, shipwrecks, wars – and maps:

> There are other words for the places I have gone indelibly.
> A kinder geographer would unstitch names from borders,
> dismantle the legends and maps.
> — 'PRODIGAL ANIMALS'

What is sought is language and thought which is 'gorgeous', to use a favourite word of Mei-en's – 'I was gorgeous / in anger. Drop dead' ('Ariel'); 'gorgeous and brutal unshod / grace' ('Man O' War'); 'May the meek inherit / something gorgeous' ('The Extinction Diaries: Psalm'). Its use may be a nod to Frank O'Hara's 'You are Gorgeous and I'm Coming'. She has the same exuberance of tone as O'Hara. And like him, she is fond of the vocative 'O!'

Yearling is replete with motifs from fairy tales and children's books – notably in her 'Pinnochia' poems. Mei-en states: 'Received narratives and voices are, for me, as perversely, gorgeously full of potential as are received forms like the sonnet or sestina. They are ancient like a religious ritual is ancient.' The emigrant experience – travelling to a new land, becoming other – is central. In 'Pinnochia from Pleasure Island', the narrator asks, 'Where did I grow up, get out'; her family is 'buck / -shot spat from out the mouth of a motherland'. The gun terminology has echoes of Emily Dickinson's 'My Life had stood – a Loaded Gun': 'Where I come from / would I go back? / If yes, reload me'; 'I am target / shot, spat out from the mouth of a mother'. 'This is Siren Country' is a poem of emigrant 'mythic passage' and family, and extends the gun imagery:

> And hail to the mother and father you never knew
> we had. To you, no generation walked on water
>
> before us, so we sing down the family tree and cast
> original seed. We are armada. We are cannon.

In 'Taxi, Singapore, Ohio', she further interrogates ideas of home. Mei-en has spoken of 'a language barrier between myself and my grandparents' generation, which has to do with my feelings of utter failure when it comes to making art about my family with language'. In this poem she seeks the 'words / that could have taken us home nowhere', and notes 'the next life will be landlocked', as her taxi driver grandfather 'turns left on red / forever'.

The colour red is a constant. We have 'the strange, red swell of a barn / swallow's belly' ('Ephemera'); 'the red eye-fruit of the mirabelle / tree'

('Rough Husbandry'); 'A red illumination to light the animal amen' (*Canis lupus familiar song of songs*'); and 'a red-throated rapture' ('Era for Drowning'). 'I don't think of sounds as coloured unless I'm feeling corrupt', wrote Frank O'Hara. Mei-en has suggested that 'colour is a useful starting point from which to explore difference, given how often synaesthesia is referenced among poets ... This brings us back to the question of the body in writing, for tics, compulsions, and synaesthetic experiences are all transgressive bodily experiences.'

These poems are about the formation of a consciousness, and about the poet observing that process: 'Once, I saw the alarming & cooled heart of myself' ('Through a Glass through Which We Cannot See'); 'new and electric in the deadened / of night' ('Era for Drowning'). There's a ferocious incantatory drive to many of the poems, with biblical cadences and echoes. Her 'Pinnochia' poems touch on what creates a person, and in 'Prodigal Animals' she evokes 'a minor world, emergent, its language mine'. Mei-en's poetry is elemental – motifs of earth, wind, fire and water abound. 'I have been lit', she writes. Her poetry is fiery and fierce, true to form but wildly imaginative. Her just published collection *The Bees Make Money in the Lion* is a roller-coaster ride through alien landscapes, skewed science fictional yarns, American capitalism and racism, lyrical androids, bees talking, and what have you. Lo Kwa Mei-en is a major voice who richly rewards rereading – her poetry is simply *gorgeous*.

Anna Journey is a poet of a very different stripe. Her first two collections, *If Birds Gather Your Hair for Nesting* and *Vulgar Remedies*, were noted for their lush imagery and claustrophobic atmospheres. Her Southern Gothic poems are short stories in miniature, set against the landscapes of Mississippi, Florida and Texas. She recalls 'the fanciest / / hotel in Richmond' (the Confederate capital), 'with its old / Deco fountain in the lobby / where pet alligators swam circles / through the Jazz Age'. Journey has lived in Richmond, with 'its Civil War cobblestones showing through the cracks underfoot'. Her shaggy-dog stories are populated by 'Virginia politicians and Baptist preachers' ('Upon Asking the Cashier at Kroger to Scan That Old Tattoo of a Barcode on My Forearm'), blues singers, a 'cokehead gravedigger', peeping toms and southern belles.

Journey aligns herself with Beckian Fritz Goldberg, and praises her 'bold associations, her startling images, her irreverent tones, and her interest in fusing lyrical beauty within realms of the grotesque'. Journey's latest collection, *The Atheist Wore Goat Silk*, also locates poetry in history and personal memory. 'I've got classical myths, family stories, Appalachian spells', she says. Like Mei-en, there's a potent sense the poems are told by a singular voice. They are intimate, conversational, they recall adolescence and family secrets, as in 'Bloodlines':

> Each time
> I visit my childhood home, I walk
>
> through the hallway's fogged
> portraits to the steaming kitchen,
>
> where the pot's metal alloy
> smells like blood filling the house.

Her closeted, gay, former psychiatrist grandfather is a recurring figure throughout Journey's books. He resurfaces in 'Bloodlines', 'sunk toward the hard // lip of his highball glass every night / since his best friend from med school // shot himself'. Journey's decadent images nod to Baudelaire's erotic 'language of flowers' – 'The devil prises open my red hibiscus like skirts' (from *If Birds Gather Your Hair for Nesting*) ; 'shrines / to the stunted relics of Texan magnolias' ('Past Life Evaporation Riff'); and 'the fuchsia bougainvillea unpurses / its dry lips, licks the sweat / from my neck' ('The Atheist Wore Goat Silk').

As with Mei-en, Journey is concerned with the body – notably the body transformed by wounds. In 'Accidental Blues Voice', an ex-lover's voice is transformed by a skiing mishap in which a ski pole punctures his vocal chords: 'his pink throat skewered like Saint / Sebastian or the raw quiver of his Greek father's / peppered lamb kebobs'. There's a pet cat brain-damaged by a crochet hook; and, at a sleepover, a teenage girl has her eye accidentally stepped on by a friend. The body also is mapped:

> You walk wearing
>
> a different darkness than mine, that whole
> parched region on your back.
> – 'TO THE PEEPING TOM WHO DISGUISED HIMSELF AS AN OKLAHOMA NIGHT'
>
> Mole on my shoulder. Road map
> of the whole damn state
> of Texas.
> – 'ASYMMETRICAL'

Journey's poems occupy a liminal space of sinister swamps, decaying Confederate graveyards and sleazy motels, places where nights are heavy, humid – 'The air's pores clogged with menthol', 'the white oak swamp's / wafts of methane'. She writes of talismanic objects – prom dresses, crazy quilts, stuffed animals, even a Victorian chamber pot. Scent is often the avenue to memory: 'The scent of the jasmine comes in heavy / as a past life' ('Past Life Evaporation Riff'). Her narrator is restless, insomniac, she '[walks] from room / to room' ('Nocturnal Activity'). As in David Lynch's films, Journey's suburban America is both creepy and comic – take 'Lucifer's Panties at Lowe's Garden Center' (from *If Birds Gather Your Hair for Nesting*):

> I told the serial killer he could feed his Venus flytrap Spam
> > the summer I worked the outdoor lawn
>
> and garden center. I'd known to say this since fifteen, with my mother telling me
> > all men who ask young girls directions
> from their white vans are murderers.

For all the density in her work, Journey's voice is frequently sassy, direct. There's a film noir sensibility at work – hence the cinematic immediacy of an image like 'Pimp's-hat shadows in the flowering date palm' (from *If Birds Gather Your Hair for Nesting*). Her use of short lines, couplets and tercets allows her narratives to breathe on the page. If at times she veers too close to the whimsical – as in the throwaway poem 'The Dildophone' – she remains a poet whose best work fuses baroque imagery with honed storytelling, leading the reader into realms of seductive grotesquerie.

Thomas McCarthy

LAST SERVICE IN THE ORTHODOX SYNAGOGUE

It was a soft day in Israel and more than a last Shabbat
When all the published pages of young David Marcus came apart

And fell again as vellum droplets of Cork rain. I looked
Back with undiminished love at the quires David made –

Even the last wet moon wore the courtesy of a yarmulka.
It's not that our days have been young and fiery, but this day

Was as old as the seams on Maurice Hurwitz's fawn coat.
Maurice, I miss you. But you would surely have come

With me. We might have been alone together the way
Friends can halve a lonely apartness, that feeling after

You've had to hide who you are. A London Rabbi told you how
They had machines beyond Ireland, new machines for killing

Jews. "Ah, Europe, the end of our beginning," your father said.
We sing 'The Banks of My Own Lovely Lee' in Hebrew as all shuffle

Through the door. Your scrolls will be sent elsewhere; there will be
Nobody left to remember. As Cork's barley-sugar melts in my pocket

I cross the iron bridge that was named by Mayor Goldberg and think,
Again, how this disturbed world still has important negative

Consequences for Jews. Ah, look here; grey rain for relief, the soft
Cork rain that fell for a century upon uncollated Irish leaves.

Laura Webb

SUBJECTIVITY

I liked the way you said Battle of the Boyne
and how you knew who the relevant Kings were
and how when you pronounced their names
they came out of your mouth in *italics*.

And I liked how Drogheda was twinned with Salinas
in California, and told you about María of the same name
and how she was one of the most loyal friends
to Catherine of Aragon whilst she waited for Henry to love her

or so history records. And on nights like this
I like to think of all the twin towns out under their various
moons, communicating in secret tones, attending
language schools, and of Drogheda seen from space,

much the same as Drogheda seen from space
four hundred years ago, should anyone have noticed.

John Kinsella

THE GALE LIFTS THE ROOF OFF THE 90,000 LITRE TANK

We hear a *whoowoowoo* and *all-stop* – wondering
where it comes from, trees bending to touch
the ground, rain cauterising the house.

It sounds like violence in the fireplace, says Tracy,
as the wind plays havoc with flame, with the reinforced
firebox. I fight the door and step outside to piece

the scene together, and notice a segment of the tank's tin roof
straining against the gale which will complete its lift
imminently. We are all part of the gale, we all have chunks

of agency ripped away. We are all watched while performing
survival, animate inanimate in all classifications of life.
Kingdoms rise, kingdoms fall, and the wind's hand adds

another category to the five of living things we acknowledge,
though twists a way into all matter, and works down
seven levels, trumpeting a personalised origin of species.

So I climb at a tangent to the tank's collar as Tracy keeps watch,
and wrestle the tin lid back into the circular, make diameter
snug to the plane, discoid click into circumference, unopening

the can – but likewise I yell into the gale as the porthole-frame
snaps at my wrist. Chaos of lift and warp, shape and pattern, bloody
signing off. The ladder will fall. We will retreat inside. Nurse my wounds.

Kevin Cantwell

AN ESSAY ON TYPOGRAPHY

      Hopkins would say they *fettled* these flecks of light from alloy
as steel dust – these jewellers who cut letters of type from stock.
      With a bird's tongue file, they shaved the burrs and nicked
the chaff they puffed aside to make the slant front display
      a book hand meant to imitate Petrarch's script.
They set without kerning one wavering page of *Nature*
      wedged in a proofing tray by wood-block *furniture*
and shimmed *quoins* – but first they waved each glyph
      through candle flame, smoke-pressed it onto wet paper.
One apprentice touched a hot italic to his forearm,
      and his inky boy, so cold, so soon, so this forewarns,
in their rooms above where the town's rank sluice would fall and disappear,
      let his fingernail, in a chipped polish dubbed Purple Seed,
pick the scab to make the letter bleed.

Eavan Boland

BRIGIT PEGEEN KELLY (1951-2016)

Brigit Pegeen Kelly's death in October 2016 took away one of the finest living poets. Her three books offer exemplary work. In poem after poem she displays a rare ability to complicate the lyric. She fashions a speaker who resists becoming a self. She pushes her poems towards a hermetic zeal no one had visited with more purpose since Emily Dickinson. The American poet Stephen Dobyns expressed what many felt when he described her as 'one of the very best poets now writing in the United States. In fact, there is no one who is any better.'

And yet there was an odd, almost eerie silence around her death. As if no one could hit on an accurate language to describe her loss. When news came of her passing – a surprise to everyone – social media filled with a keen, shocked sense of her absence. But the comments were mostly personal – remembrances especially of her inspiring kindness as a teacher. And little else. Brigit Pegeen Kelly was an honoured poet. She had won prizes, been cited for her work and was widely admired. Nevertheless, the sort of analysis that follows on a significant artist's death – that records an achievement and sets the terms of its transmission – was missing.

Some of the reason may lie in the difficulty of fixing her in a category. She was elusive. Even her influences were hard to pin down. When Kelly came to Stanford a few years ago – as Lane lecturer in the Creative Writing program – she mentioned her plan for the evening's event. More than half the reading, she told us, would be from Wallace Stevens' work; the rest would be her own. We managed to dissuade her. People would travel to the reading we explained, and would be eager to hear her.

There is a clue in her turning to Stevens. Not simply that he was a favourite poet. It was more than that. Stevens was a poet who had constructed a signature speaker, one whose authority was not immediately traceable. In the actions and events of works as different as 'The Emperor of Ice Cream' and 'The River of Rivers in Connecticut', questions ghost the periphery of his poems. Is this the poet speaking? Is this a fiction? Is it both?

Certainly the speaker of a Stevens poem is hardly ever the familiar social self of mid-century American poetry. There is no neighbourly weather in a Stevens poem as there is in Ginsberg's 'A Supermarket in California' or Robert Lowell's 'The Drinker' or Elizabeth Bishop's 'The Moose'. Instead there is a voice coming from no exact moment, no definable place.

A voice never out of the poet's control: moving in and out of music and statement, ready to steal meaning and yet not satisfied with it. The same could be said of Kelly. In this way, Stevens may have provided shelter for her own wayward project.

Brigit Pegeen Kelly was born in Palo Alto, California in 1951. She grew up in Indiana. But actual details of her life – even in our noisy culture – are hard to come by. She married and had three children. A note in a 1987 journal she contributed to reports that she was then living on a farm in New Jersey and working for a children's literary magazine. After that there is little enough. She avoided both interviews and self-revealing critiques. She was utterly uninterested in fame. To reverse FR Leavis' unkind comment about the Sitwells – that they belonged to the history of publicity and not poetry – she belonged to poetry and shunned publicity. Even the garrulous and informative Wikipedia is forced to resort to anti-biographical statement when describing her. 'An intensely private woman', it says, 'little is known about her life.'

I did know Brigit Pegeen Kelly. Not well, certainly, but enough in our few meetings to have a strong impression of her. We first met one evening in Vermont when we were both spending some weeks at the Bread Loaf conference. She was a tall, graceful woman, with an oval face and a mercurial sense of humour that took time to reveal itself. Her presence was quiet and she was not sociable. But in a classroom a wonderful geniality emerged and was freely given to her students.

After the evening readings we sometimes walked back together. Our resident houses were side by side at the end of a starless path. It was cold. But the porches were sheltered and we stood talking on those unseasonable Vermont nights as the light went out of the distance and the mountain disappeared. I remember a spider to the side of the porch, descending and rising again on some inexplicable platform and how it amused her. We went to each other's classes and readings. We talked every day. Yet after her death I was bemused to remember that hardly any of our conversations had touched on poetry.

She brought out three books between 1987 and 2004. The first, *To The Place of Trumpets*, was published by Yale University Press. James Merrill, who chose her as the Yale Younger Poet that year, wrote in his preface about the rich tension between faith and not-faith in her work. 'Free of the shaping past?' he asks. 'Isn't the most we can do, to be free *with* it, submit it to some shaping of our own? This freedom in any case I find especially heartening in Kelly's poems. Far from leading to negation or bitterness, her lost faith becomes the stuff of vision'.

But it was a vision that could be skewed. Given the sheer reach of her language, it's possible to overlook how dark Kelly's arguments could be. A deep pessimism about the human will and human behaviour pervades her work. One poem in the book points this up. It's called 'Imagining Their Own Hymns', and is voiced by a young girl. Her mood is sullen. She resents her church. She resents the so-called kind women who provide her with charity.

As the poem goes on the speaker becomes less realistic. Her tone gathers power, becoming a symbolist transport for a vision of spiritual perversion she could never have had in real life. This will become a familiar manoeuvre in a Kelly poem. Vision will be provided just as often by the forces of darkness as those of light. In the final lines, the girl lands a magic-making anger – as well as her hopes of escape – on the figures of the church angels.

> And these angels that the women turn to
> are not good either. They are sick of Jesus,
> who never stops dying, hanging there white
> and large, his shadow blue as pitch, and blue
> the bruise on his chest, with spread petals,
> like the hydrangea blooms I tear from
> Mrs. Macht's bush and smash on the sidewalk.
> One night they will get out of here. One night
> when the weather is turning cold and a few
> candles burn, they will leave St. Blase standing
> under his canopy of glass lettuce
> and together, as in a wedding march,
> their pockets full of money from the boxes
> for the sick poor, they will walk down the aisle,
> imagining their own hymns, past the pews
> and the water fonts in which small things float,
> down the streets of our narrow town, while
> the bells ring and the birds fly up in the fields
> beyond – and they will never come back.

In 1995 Kelly's second book was published by BOA Editions, simply titled *Song*. It was immediately successful. *To the Place of Trumpets* had shown rare gifts of syntax and timing. Kelly's characteristic line was talky, uncluttered, and yet had a clear and sophisticated musical intent. All of this had progressed in *Song* into bold themes and images. The title poem was eye-catching. She had published it two years earlier in *The Southern Review*. Its presence was immediately obvious in the new volume, where it was placed first – a spacious, shadowy piece taking up all the oxygen.

The poem is mysterious and strangely plotted: A goat has its head cut off by schoolboys. The goat's head is hung in a tree and begins to sing. The goat has belonged to a young girl who has lavished affection on it. As the poem says: 'She named / The goat Broken Thorn Sweet Blackberry, named it after / The night's bush of stars, because the goat's silky hair / Was dark as well water, because it had eyes like wild fruit.'

The action of the boys is both strange and symbolist. The language shimmers with suggestion and insinuation. The goat is not quite real. The severed head and body have mystical longings. 'The head called to the body. The body to the head. / They missed each other. The missing grew large between them, / Until it pulled the heart right out of the body, until / The drawn heart flew toward the head, flew as a bird flies / Back to its cage and the familiar perch from which it trills.'

Dissonant as 'Song' is, for many people it announced an extraordinary arrival in American poetry. A reviewer from the journal *The American Poet* wrote 'Her poems are like no one else's – hard and luminous, weird in the sense of making a thing strange that we at last might see it'. But the masterpiece of 'Song' is the final poem: 'Three Cows and the Moon'. It is a deceptive, untidy pastoral – a mother and two children playing baseball in fading light – and it is wrapped around its own careful disorder. Even the darkness is disorderly. The speaker tells us she heard how darkness behaves differently from what we thought. It doesn't come down but rather rises up: 'It gets the ankles first. It circles / The ankles like flood water'.

Looked at closely 'Three Cows and the Moon' is an *Ars Poetica*: one of those poems that act as quiet manifestos. Eventually the game stops, the animals vanish, and the moon rises. It is high and small. It might be a flower the poem suggests. It might be an oracle. The final lines of the poem could be a summary of the core of Kelly's work: a description of the moon as 'Something / Completely understood. But unspeakable.'

Her third book, *The Orchard*, appeared nine years later in 2004. It was a graver, darker enterprise. The poems were less lyrical, the lines longer. Frequently the texts tilted over into heraldic prose arguments. The animals were now more assertively signs and legends. She-wolves and satyrs filled the pages. In the title poem – a long complex meditation on violence – a dog eats a doe, at first in a dream, then in reality. The speaker picks up an apple to throw at the dog and finds herself holding not an apple, 'But the still warm and almost beating / Heart of some holy being'.

It was at Bread Loaf that I first saw Brigit Pegeen Kelly read, one evening late. The room was crowded. As usual, she read some poems by Wallace Stevens. Then one of her own. Perhaps it was more than one. But this single poem is what I remember.

It was called 'Closing Time; Iskandariya' – Iskandariya is the old name for Alexandria, the ancient city that stood between Babylon and Seleucia. In ancient times it was also the site of the great library referred to in the last line. 'Closing Time; Iskandariya' was never published in full book form. It appeared as an op-ed in the *New York Times* in 2005. It can be read at this distance as a culmination of many of Kelly's themes. The poem sprawls across the page, prosy and dense. It seems to say at last what she wanted to say in so many poems: about human will and submission and the perversions of grace itself. In her actual reading the argument went forward with speed and precision. Her listeners that night, myself included, were mesmerized by the sheer scope of it. But the poem rewards a slower study of its elaborate build and conclusion.

The poem begins: 'It was not a scorpion I asked for, I asked for a fish, but maybe God misheard my request'. As the speaker continues, lost in a world that seems half-fable, half-prayer, the scorpion emerges as an unlikely ally in helping the speaker understand the blindness of human purpose. 'God gave me a scorpion, a venomous creature, to be sure, a bug with the bite of Cleopatra's asp, but not, as I soon found out, despite the dark gossip, a lover of violence or a hater of men. In truth, it is shy, the scorpion, a creature with eight eyes and almost no sight, who shuns the daylight, and is driven mad by fire'.

How are we to read Brigit Pegeen Kelly? After her death I kept returning to a conversation we had at Stanford when she came as a visitor. We were in a coffee shop on campus, spring light filtering through every window. She spoke lightly – almost off-handedly – of wanting to suppress her first book. She was not satisfied with the work in it.

I'm not sure how intent she was on this. But the conversation itself pushed me towards other reflections. I thought her poetry was untroubled in its reach and confidence; but her attitude to it less so. In conversation it was clear that she considered herself an exile in a world of expression. She was – though it seems strange to say it – only reluctantly a poet. It wasn't just that she disdained much of the poetry world's traffic. Although she did. (And yet she found a warm and deeply supportive publisher in Michael Schmidt of Carcanet, by whose kind permission 'Song' is reprinted here). Nevertheless, the readings, the gossip, the fray were not for her. It was also that she clearly longed for a world less governed by the limits of language, more amenable to the freedoms of silence. She mentioned to me at one point that when she was young she had considered the religious life, but hadn't committed to it.

Was she then a religious poet? Could it be that our losing that critical vocabulary – which we have long lost – helps to account for the difficulty in talking about her achievement? I'm not sure. She doesn't read like a religious poet. The conventional religious poet writes poems of doubt from a perspective of faith. But as her poems progress, her work does something different: it tracks through spaces of broken statues, violated animals, and disorderly perceptions. In this trajectory, she seems more like an elegist for faith than an owner of it.

But there is another way of understanding her work – and maybe a more accurate one. And that is through the history of twentieth-century poetry itself. In this context, it often seemed to me she stood on the wrong side of the inheritance. With the rise and fall of modernism, the experiments in surrealism, the gestures towards interiority, it could be argued that poetry failed to build a convincing architecture of the inward life. The self-reflective life, certainly. But not the contemplative one that so many of Kelly's poems seem to yearn for. And yet she remained an ardent maker of the blueprints.

Kelly's poems are stocked with wild creatures – with blind scorpions and headless goats, with angels pushing down the street of a small town. These are first and foremost poetic figures. But they can also be seen as emblems of that contemplative life a turbulent poetic century had turned out of its habitat. Kelly's work registers that twentieth-century failure – that inability of poetry to speak the dialect of the contemplative life. Her best poems – like 'Closing Time; Iskandariya' – seem to register her striving to find points of connection with a lost peace. From that striving come the powerful, exemplary poems that survived the loss. And will remain.

Brigit Pegeen Kelly

SONG

Listen: there was a goat's head hanging by ropes in a tree.
All night it hung there and sang. And those who heard it
Felt a hurt in their hearts and thought they were hearing
The song of a night bird. They sat up in their beds, and then
They lay back down again. In the night wind, the goat's head
Swayed back and forth, and from far off it shone faintly
The way the moonlight shone on the train track miles away
Beside which the goat's headless body lay. Some boys
Had hacked its head off. It was harder work than they had imagined.
The goat cried like a man and struggled hard. But they
Finished the job. They hung the bleeding head by the school
And then ran off into the darkness that seems to hide everything.
The head hung in the tree. The body lay by the tracks.
The head called to the body. The body to the head.
They missed each other. The missing grew large between them,
Until it pulled the heart right out of the body, until
The drawn heart flew toward the head, flew as a bird flies
Back to its cage and the familiar perch from which it trills.
Then the heart sang in the head, softly at first and then louder,
Sang long and low until the morning light came up over
The school and over the tree, and then the singing stopped ...
The goat had belonged to a small girl. She named
The goat Broken Thorn Sweet Blackberry, named it after
The night's bush of stars, because the goat's silky hair
Was dark as well water, because it had eyes like wild fruit.
The girl lived near a high railroad track. At night
She heard the trains passing, the sweet sound of the train's horn
Pouring softly over her bed, and each morning she woke
To give the bleating goat his pail of warm milk. She sang
Him songs about girls with ropes and cooks in boats.
She brushed him with a stiff brush. She dreamed daily
That he grew bigger, and he did. She thought her dreaming
Made it so. But one night the girl didn't hear the train's horn,
And the next morning she woke to an empty yard. The goat
Was gone. Everything looked strange. It was as if a storm

Had passed through while she slept, wind and stones, rain
Stripping the branches of fruit. She knew that someone
Had stolen the goat and that he had come to harm. She called
To him. All morning and into the afternoon, she called
And called. She walked and walked. In her chest a bad feeling
Like the feeling of the stones gouging the soft undersides
Of her bare feet. Then somebody found the goat's body
By the high tracks, the flies already filling their soft bottles
At the goat's torn neck. Then somebody found the head
Hanging in a tree by the school. They hurried to take
These things away so that the girl would not see them.
They hurried to raise money to buy the girl another goat.
They hurried to find the boys who had done this, to hear
Them say it was a joke, a joke, it was nothing but a joke ...
But listen: here is the point. The boys thought to have
Their fun and be done with it. It was harder work than they
Had imagined, this silly sacrifice, but they finished the job,
Whistling as they washed their large hands in the dark.
What they didn't know was that the goat's head was already
Singing behind them in the tree. What they didn't know
Was that the goat's head would go on singing, just for them,
Long after the ropes were down, and that they would learn to listen,
Pail after pail, stroke after patient stroke. They would
Wake in the night thinking they heard the wind in the trees
Or a night bird, but their hearts beating harder. There
Would be a whistle, a hum, a high murmur, and, at last, a song,
The low song a lost boy sings remembering his mother's call.
Not a cruel song, no, no, not cruel at all. This song
Is sweet. It is sweet. The heart dies of this sweetness.

Diarmuid Johnson

NÍ FUATH LINN

Céasadh an fear ar an gcrois
Ní namhaid linn an crann dá réir
Ní fuath linn an t-adhmad.
Cuireadh na tairní trína dhá láimh
Ní namhaid linn gach bior dá réir
Ní fuath linn gach díreach.
Roinneadh an brat gan chiumhais
Ní namhaid linn gach roinnt ó shin
Ní fuath linn gach leathrud.
An leathrud ní fuath linn
Ainneoin céasadh fir ar chrois
Ní fuath linn an t-adhmad ná an chraobh.

Diarmuid Johnson

NEAD DREOILÍN

Scríobh mé litir chuig an rí;

'Boladh céire ar maidin
 Staighre ard san oíche;
 Ní iarraim ort ach an dá ní sin'.

D'fhreagair an corónach mé;

'Bronnaim sin ort,' ar sé, 'a fhir gan díon,'
'Ach freagair dhom an cheist seo.'

'Cé méid bliain nead dreoilín á tógáil?
 Cé méid bliain an t-éan beag á fí go glic?
 Cé méid bliain dó á síorchóiriú go gobach, grinn?'

Scríobh mé litir chuig an rí.

Diarmuid Johnson

NÍ FÉIDIR COILL A CHUR

Is rud gan chleití
A bheas i sochraid na coille.

Agus nuair a chuirfeas an bháisteach uirthi
A léine mhór, mhín
Éagfaidh an ciúnas féin.

Rud gan chleití, rud gan uaigh, rud gan reilg
A bheas i sochraid na coille.

Mar ní sa talamh atá an uaigh
Ní sa bhfód atá reilg na gcrann
Níl cónra ar domhan i gcóir na bpréamh
Ná eileatram ar bith chomh fada leis an gcraobh.

Ach caoinfidh an fharraige an choill
Caoinfidh farraige ama an crann, an bláth agus an ghéag.

Nífidh an fharraige cosa na coille
Leathfaidh sí a braillín ar an trá.

Agus codlóidh cnámha na seanchoille
Codlóidh siad faoin mbrat sáile gan chiumhais gan snáth.

Codlóidh an choill gan chónra gan uaigh
Mar coill ní féidir, ní féidir coill a chur.

Michael Hofmann

BUNCH OF FIVES

Paul Muldoon, *Selected Poems* (Faber and Faber/Farrar, Straus and Giroux, 2016) hb £14.99 / $27.

There is almost no getting around it: any real devotee of a poet will be a completist, and a 'selected poems' to such a reader will be a ho-hum affair. (Perhaps it's that the poet, ranging and choosing, 'playing god', has usurped the job of the reader, and the reader – the good reader, the ideal reader – resents him for it). A loveless and friendless book, then, by and large, bespeaking at the most the poet's good or bad judgment, his self-infatuation or self-severity, a weakness for his beginnings, or a preference for the newer stuff. It will be obvious or perverse, both too long and too short (more is less, but less is less as well), neither old nor new, and the whole thing standard, predictable and expressionless.

Not so this one of Paul Muldoon's. The astonishing escapologist ('Who cooked and ate an omelette/ midway across Niagara falls?' he asks in the teasing poem autobiography called 'A Collegelands Catechism'), has basically done it again, and by the simplest means. He has represented each one of his now 12 books – from *New Weather* (1973) to *One Thousand Things Worth Knowing* (2015) – with five poems apiece. From the eight poems of *Madoc: A Mystery* (1990) – five pieces; from the forty-two of *Hay* (1998) – five pieces. The Irish landscape painting on the cover of the US edition (Martin Gale's *Dividing Road*), a milk and water sky in late winter or early spring, tufty yellow grass, a couple of shaggy vealers, a shiny motorway curving emptily away into the distance, itself is horizontally sliced five ways. Sixty poems, a little over two hundred pages, and strait-jacketed by the *Zwang* to quincunx, a gift to old and new readers alike. As often with Muldoon, one wonders why no one has thought to do something similar before. (I can't think of anything quite like it).

And the magic five? Just a lovely bundle, the Roman V, four sticks and the diagonal, odd, prime, Fibonacci. The *règle* of this particular Procrustean *jeu*. Given the perfectly unreasonable, non-negotiable five – just *five* – who could blame the poet for choosing one five over another, or another? It's just the number of basketball players that happen to be on court at any one time. There's always the bench. And the coach. Heck, even Muldoon's 'A' and 'B' teams, even his apprentices and trainees, will run rings round the senior outfits of just about anyone now writing (it's a little embarrassing). No 'Elizabeth', no 'Blemish', no 'Holy Thursday', no 'Gold', no 'Profumo', no 'The Right Arm', no 'The Wishbone', no 'Sushi', no '7, Middagh Street', no 'The Train', no 'They That Wash on Thursday', and on and on and on, to mention just a few of my own favourites. And yet. And yet.

The *Selected* shows a poet, who, in spite of the wildest and most unpredictable changes – once he was a reed, now he's a redwood forest – has always been himself. He seems never to have written a line that anyone else – and least of all his imitators – could have written, that was not utterly distinctive. Always the slightly mocking or teasing use of idiom; always the dreaming ear, coming up with cognates or false cognates (I thought of going through the book for all the words that begin with 'q'!), rhymes and false rhymes and barely-at-all rhymes; always the characteristic Muldoon drive and earnest sense of purpose, even or especially when a poem begins – apparently – in a blizzard of footnotes or a thicket of encumbrances or adversatives. The masterful patience. The toyings with genres and forms. The variations on the sonnet, from trim to shaggy to the never-to-be-forgotten '*Just / throw/ him/ a / cake / of / Sunlight / soap, / let / him / wash / him- /self / ashore*', from the long poem written in sonnets, 'The More a Man Has the More a Man Wants' in *Quoof* of 1983 (there's a q-word!). A love of spuriousness, and then again a fondness for direct utterance. Often, and here maybe increasingly, the use of literary tags and other found materials, a kind of compositional recycling, old wine into the new bottles, and all tuned and played like a glockenspiel.

Sampling from the successive books as they occurred also shows one something like their biographical humility or rootedness: every one of them hangs on or revolves around a major life-event, a bereavement, a separation, a move from one country to another, the birth of a child, an anniversary. More than ever, it seems ridiculous – scandalous, even – to say, as I think the Merton Professor of English once did, that Muldoon is not 'about' anything, is cold, fanciful, flippant, lacking in feeling, and to play him off against Heaney. Rather, in terms once devised by Dylan Thomas and that I once thought stupid, but that now seem to me incredibly helpful, a Muldoon poem is always both towards words and away from words. It is both paint and likeness, tone and tune, abstract and concrete, lexical and self-evident. In the manner of the best contemporary poetry – which of course Muldoon has been instrumental in constructing – it is rich, intricate and unassuming.

Some time, over time, Muldoon morphed from being an ironic and superior provincial to an ironic and superior cosmopolitan, adding a 'mixed marriage' of his own, to the Jewish-American writer Jean Hanff Korelitz (solemnized in the long, riotous but endlessly moving poem, 'At the Sign of the Black Horse, September 1999', about the flooded Raritan Canal in front of the poet's onetime house in Hopewell, New Jersey, in the wake of Hurricane Floyd, but sooner or later about everything), to that of his Armagh parents; telling us (in 'A Hare at Aldergrove') 'how my own DNA is 87% European and East Asian 13%'. From being barely referential at all, if anything Kavanagh-local, he switched to poems that seem half upper-case, exotic cocktails of arcana, suave quandaries or stammerings of fact, or in the words of one recent title, 'Dirty Data'. Irish, Jewish and American words and sounds and figures are put in the blender. 'Pecs and abs, Lew, abs and pecs.' A poem is a hallucination, a synthesis, a *carambolage*. Animals, continents, etymologies go into its making. I've long thought that perhaps Muldoon's overriding quality is that he's easily bored. It seems as though, in a terror of merely coasting or repeating himself (as if!), he's gone on adding dimensions.

And yet something like simplicity persists. Or close to it. The punning 'Pelt' is a brief lyric written in plain words and short lines, with full couplet rhymes (the others, admittedly, wobble across the stanzas in the now familiar Muldoon way), beginning with a rain shower, imagining or remembering a funeral, and ending with 'a contentment / I'd not felt in years, / not since that winter / I'd worn the world / against my skin, / worn it fur side in'. 'The Old Country' is fancier, a crown of sonnets, in readymade phrases or wonderful mis-manufactures of clichés, but delivered with such intimate understanding of and contemptuous, diagnostic fury against those of his countrymen who are stuck and unevolving and deceitful and craven that the MacNeice of 'Valediction' would have been proud of it:

> Every runnel was a Rubicon
> where every ditch was a last ditch.
> Every man was 'a grand wee mon'
> whose every pitch was another sales pitch
>
> now every boat was a burned boat.
> Every cap was a cap in hand.
> Every coat a trailed coat.
> Every band was a gallant band
>
> across the broken bridge
> and broken ridge after broken ridge
> where you couldn't beat a stick with a big stick.
>
> Every straight road was a straight up speed trap.
> Every decision was a snap.
> Every cut was a cut to the quick.

The mythos and the fatuousness of Ireland are held in suspense; the romance and the abjection; the panache and the threadbare cringe. And it is all a game. Or rather, at this stage, is only playing at being a game.

Leontia Flynn

28

Government servants with your dinky backpacks,
cohorts of bullshit, at its beck and call:
friend-of-my-youth, and you, my bosom buddy,
how is it going? Have you had your fill
of corporate wine and state-subsidized hunger
fiddled expenses, claim forms and books cooked
to show some profit? Ah, well I remember,
back in my time, I also cooked the books
for a boss – who then proceeded to bend me down
and slowly, but systematically, fuck me over
while being simultaneously in turn,
yes, thoroughly shafted by *his* manager ...
an even bigger cock. God help us all
taught thus to aspire to the 'professional' classes:
what blots on humanity. May they rot in hell.

Jean O'Brien

THE MOST EXPENSIVE HEN HOUSE IN ENGLAND

> *It's rumoured that a 'lost' Francis Bacon painting was in fact discarded by the artist after a stay at St Ives, and was subsequently used to roof a hen house.*

I am a fat contented hen, when I am happy
I lay big brown eggs, the yoke and albumen liquid
gold and viscous, under claw the straw is soft
and warm, my eggs flourish there. The farmer
is a neat natty woman, her black hair pulled back
in a bun, nothing flashy. Her linen apron holds all sorts
of titbits and tasty morsels. She dips her plump hands
into her apron and scatters seeds and treats.

Monday of the bad wind, the roof of our shed lifted
and floated off, my feathered sisters and I spent the night
in a funk, *cluck clucking* fearful of the stinking fox,
he could hop in and grab any one of us
in his chops and no one could save us. We cowed
in a huddle and never slept a wink. The farmer
was all aflap about our predicament and set
to getting us a new roof, pulled a tarpaulin over us
for safety while she searched St Ives for a replacement.

She went up the town to the painters' house by the sea,
She thought they were a 'quare' lot in there, heard
tales of drink and debauchery, whatever that might be.
The landlady stood by the door, her arms full of canvas
squares. Said they were the scoundrel Bacon's
and he owed her. They struck a deal, fresh eggs for the month
for four large canvasses, those coloured ones would do
nicely. She lugged them home and tacked them over the coop.
Job done.

Through the day I go pecking along in the dirt, bustling in and
out of the bushes, running with my sisters around the yard.
At night when the farmer calls for us to assume our perches
we march in quick time and as darkness falls, my beady eyes
brood on our new roof. Our Bacon. I can just make out a figure,

in hues of pink and blue. It is he, all feet and elbows towering over us,
and hanging there not to be ignored, though it seems in the wrong
place, is his wattle, bright red and shining. It is magnificent,
I gaze at it and my brown eggs release.

Matthew Sweeney

TIN MINING

Instead of climbing the wooded hill
you should descend into the tin mine

that hasn't been used for twenty years.
Be sure to take a hard hat with a light

and wear hiking boots. Avoid any
attributes such as belts or braces

that could snag on any rusty metal.
You won't need to bring a canary

for this kind of mine, but bring a small
pickaxe – there's still tin there if you

can locate it. Imagine the homemade
jewellery you'd charm your woman with,

say a brooch with the old three hares
circular motif. Take a bottle of Cornish cider

and a Toby jug with your own face on it
to celebrate – howl out a local folk song,

then climb out to round up some tourists
for the dance called the Tinners' Rabbit

involving sticks and a complex rotation
you'll have to learn and teach the others,

after which you can all retire to Zennor,
and *The Tinners' Arms* to drink more,

shouting out toasts to the Queen and Duke
of Cornwall, and anyone who takes your fancy.

Katie Donovan

THE EMPTY NEST AND THE CROCODILE

Jamie McKendrick, *Selected Poems* (Faber and Faber, 2016), £12.99.
Vona Groarke, *Selected Poems* (The Gallery Press, 2016), €12.50.

Meditations on home, displacement, and the natural world are highlighted in these two volumes representing the prize-winning work of poets Jamie McKendrick and Vona Groarke. Although McKendrick is the elder by nine years, both began publishing in the 1990s and have published six volumes of poetry. Adept with form and its constraints, both are drawn, thematically, to the fragility of structure, from McKendrick's volcanoes and wrecked cars to Groarke's crumbling houses and Skyped babysitting.

McKendrick published his first collection, *The Sirocco Room*, in 1991. His latest, *Out There*, appeared in 2012. Chosen as one of the New Generation Poets, he dedicates poems to two other members of the group: the late Mick Imlah – who died tragically at the age of 52 from Motor Neurone disease – and the German-born Michael Hofmann. In fact, to read McKendrick's *Selected Poems* is to be presented with a wide fellowship of writers who play an acknowledged part in his oeuvre.

Born in Liverpool – a city he pokes eloquent fun at in 'Epithets': 'the blarney-argoted, the blitzed and blackened' – he spent time living in Italy before settling in Oxford. He has translated Italian poets Valerio Magrelli, Pier Paolo Pasolini, and Antonella Anedda; he is also the editor of *The Faber Book of 20th-Century Italian Poems*. In this *Selected Poems* we find versions of Ovid, Catullus and Montale, nods to Carlos Drummond de Andrade, Ashbery, and Machado, and settings about as far away from 'hovel-haunted' Liverpool as one can imagine: Barcelona; Stockholm; Rome.

He is drawn to scenes of vulnerability, often historical, occasionally personal. 'The Vulcanologist', about the seventeenth-century Jesuit Athanasius exploring Vesuvius, 'like a bug on a thread', is laid out on the page in the shape of the fiery-hearted mountain itself. 'Ancient History' (from *The Marble Fly*, 1997) shows how paranoia has always been with us: 'Violence was only curbed / by belief in a rumour that the tribes / to the east had joined forces [...] The year ended fraught with the fear of war.'

Particularly powerful is his rendition of the isolation of Roger Casement in 'When Casement Crossed the Line' (from *Crocodiles and Obelisks*, 2007). Abandoned by Conrad, his good name smeared by the deliberate circulation of the notorious Black Diaries, Casement is washed up on Banna Strand where he sacrifices himself for his fellows one last time. The outrages Casement exposed in the rubber plantations of 'Leopold's Congo' are depicted in keen and crafted phrases that contain a harrowing specificity:

'wounds, / weals and keloids from the rhino-hide whip ... the dark, dry harvest of severed hands'.

In 'Polonius', we meet McKendrick's grandfather, who advises his son not to join the Masons or wear a wig (his terrible secret being that he himself is a Mason, and he wears a wig). A small, unglamorous subject can be the take-off point for McKendrick's poems to soar. 'Tinnitus' , a nine-line gem, itemises the discrete sounds which invade the sufferer's delicate ear. The humble fly is a regular inspiration, and some of the most colourful writing is bestowed upon birds.

Like Heaney, the more creaturely his poetry, the stronger its impact. 'Right of Way' (from *Ink Stone*, 2003) features two toads who have escaped the depredations of the urban landscape and insist on crossing through the poet's house – a potent reminder of the puny trajectory of human civilisation. An early poem, 'The Agave', celebrates a plant that clings to the edge of cliffs and yet survives, 'beside the prickly pears that crouch / in their hairsuits like luscious grudges'. McKendrick, a self-confessed exile, establishes toe-holds in places meticulously described, before moving on.

In the last poem, 'The Literalist', McKendrick sides with the tactile natural world against the accepted Christian order: 'When told they'd be made into fishers of men / did it not occur to a single one / that he'd be best off staying a fisher of fish'. In 'Out There', he posits earth as our real paradise, a vision only possible from the arid viewpoint of the cosmonaut.

His use of humour, which occasionally strikes a glib or smart-aleck tone (as in the list-like 'Fly Inventory'), is more often irresistible, and presents the reader with a welcome frame for life's vicissitudes. 'Unfaded' is full of dark, compassionate wit about the tyrannies of the dead: 'The dead are villains we pretend to love'. His version of Ovid's 'Galatea and Polyphemus', where the lovelorn Cyclops mourns his loss of form due to his unrewarded ardour, is hilarious: 'Entire fleets / pass by unscathed as if I were a lighthouse. / I just forget to wreck them.'

McKendrick shows sophistication and compassion in his minutely crafted celebration of the tenacity of life, even in its humblest incarnations. His sensibility is cosmopolitan and erudite yet tender and self-deprecating. Above all, his descriptive power is breath-taking, from the lush Mezzogiorno-inspired poems through to the metaphysical ponderings of the more recent work.

Like McKendrick, Vona Groarke is well-travelled. She hails from Co Longford but has lived in the US and is now based in Manchester. Groarke's first collection, *Shale*, appeared in 1994 (her most recent is *X*, published in 2014). Her *Selected Poems* is a slimmer volume than McKendrick's (93 pages to his 150), and the appearance of the book (with no page markers showing where one volume's sample ends and the other begins), is as of a fused sequence rather than his jointed retrospective. This makes for a seamless read, but rather too short – there are only six poems from her second collection, *Other People's Houses* (1999), for example. 'Lament for Art O'Leary' – Groarke's version of Eibhlín Dubh Ní Chonaill's eighteenth century composition, published in 2008 – is not represented at all.

In Groarke's work the image of the house is central: as a symbol of a relationship; of neglect; of over-burdened responsibility; of colonial Ireland; of the émigré in a new country; and, in the most recent collection X, of absence. In a poem entitled 'Patronage' (not included in this *Selected*, from *Shale*), Groarke teases the reader with the suggestion: 'a room will always cover more than it reveals'. This double focus – of revelations and concealment, offered by the structures in which we live our lives – is to be found in many of her poems.

Groarke's eloquence is particularly to the fore in her depictions of water and swimming, as in the fine second stanza of 'To Smithereens' and the exuberance of 'Pier'. However, in certain poems she hobbles her grace notes with flat or awkward-linking phrases (as in the opening of 'Some Weather'), and occasional lines lack the fluency so much in evidence elsewhere: 'Let the worst I ever do to you be die' (from 'Aubade' in *Spindrift*, 2009).

Groarke has great formal range. She composes brief lyrics, such as the whimsical 'Wind in Trees', which opens with the line: 'Tonight the wind tries on fancy dress'. And she is equally at home with long-form poems. The run-on effect of the lines that refuse to fit in 'Imperial Measure' (from *Flight*, 2002) is a nice reflection of the bizarre excess of the luxury hotel food commandeered by the desperate men and women of 1916. She is particularly fond of the tercet, which helps to break up the rather unwieldy 138-line poem, 'Athlones' (from *Juniper Street*, 2006), where the tight lives of the townspeople are lapped by the brooding 'two-faced' river,

> holding the line between
> the Pale and Irishtown, the to-and-fro of siege
> or confiscation, dual strategies of granite and edict.

A bisected Ireland, that of the Big House and the tenant, is given a new twist in the cleverly-titled dramatic monologue 'Cuttings'. The granddaughter of a maid who was slighted by her employers returns to their former abode (the aptly named Castle Proud), now a stately home open to the public. Wielding her secateurs she takes cuttings of the plants her grandmother once admired. She has her own garden where she will plant the exotic fleur-de-lis, that ancient symbol of the ruling classes.

In terms of influence, echoes of Eavan Boland can be seen in 'The Way It Goes' and 'Imperial Measure', where talismans of domestic life as experienced by anonymous women are brought into a wider perspective on historical suffering. 'Imperial Measure' contains the arresting image of the bullet-riddled sacks in Boland's Mill covering the doomed rebels with flour like 'talced' newborns.

'The verb "to herringbone"' is a poem about a distinctive stitch that provides the reader with a metaphor for Groarke's slantwise, layered style of composition, reminiscent of the work of Eiléan Ní Chuilleanáin. A companion poem, 'Flight', evokes the playful and ambitious energy Groarke uses in her writing: 'One minute, it's ruse and colour, / the next, wingspan and whir.'

Groarke has long been a mature, distinctive presence on the Irish poetry scene, each of her collections deepening in scope and confidence. In this *Selected Poems*, we see the fairy tale quality of the early love poetry giving way to what might be termed 'the coping' – that poignant, double-edged noun / verb, from 'Windmill Hymns' – and, latterly, her fascination with flowers, still lifes and visual art.

The cover of her *Selected Poems* is a Martin Gale image of an empty nest, and one of her last poems is a vision of watching her daughter walk away into adulthood through 'ten thousand doorways'. A memorable image from McKendrick's *Selected Poems* is that of the centuries-old Egyptian crocodile, a cherished gift to the city of Seville, still standing sentinel at the gate to the Court of Orange Trees. These images suggest that, for both poets, what is valued will somehow survive, and that there is more of life worth reaching for beyond the next threshold. For readers, what may lie beyond the threshold set down by the publication of their respective *Selected Poems* is a prospect worth savouring.

FEATURED POET: SOLMAZ SHARIF

Solmaz Sharif was born in Istanbul, of Iranian parents, and came to live in the United States as a young child. She went to UC Berkeley, where she worked with the influential American poet June Jordan on Jordan's Poetry for the People project. Her MFA is from New York University. She is currently a Jones lecturer at Stanford in the Creative Writing Program.

As a Stegner Fellow at Stanford – and in my workshop for some of that time – Solmaz put the finishing touches to the remarkable and ambitious project for which she received the Fellowship. This was a series of poems based on her own enquiries into meaning and language, which prompted her, in her own words, 'to stand outside of and look into, and constantly question and interrogate the collectives that exist'.

These poems became the basis of her debut volume, *Look*, published by the distinguished Graywolf Press in July 2016. The poems alternately interrogate, subvert and refresh parts of language which have been co-opted by society, by the State, by the uncaring usage of a generation of owners.

The first poem selected here, which opens the collection, turns a fierce light on that title word: 'Look'. A word which has a military connotation undergoes a mutation, and migrates in this poem into new contexts. Braided with memories of love, of misunderstanding, of verbal carelessness, the word makes a wrenching and exemplary journey from misuse to meaning.

Look has attracted many honours: it has been a finalist for the National Book Award and for the PEN 2017 Open Book Award. It was an Editor's Choice for the *New York Times Book Review*.

The poems in *Look* are certainly political. They engage the contemporary moment in a fearless and stirring way. But that, in a sense, is only their temporal existence. Beyond that, the poems serve as an elegy for language itself, for the way words can be doomed by history, and the poet summoned to rescue them. It is this last emphasis, I believe, which is fast making *Look* one of the most influential poetry books of its generation.

– Eavan Boland

look – (*) In mine warfare, a period during which a mine circuit is receptive of an influence.
Dictionary of Military and Associated Terms,
US Department of Defense, 2007

Solmaz Sharif

LOOK

It matters what you call a thing: *Exquisite* a lover called me. *Exquisite*.

Whereas *Well, if I were from your culture, living in this country,* said the man outside the 2004 Republican National Convention, *I would put up with that for this country;*

Whereas I felt the need to clarify: *You would put up with TORTURE, you mean* and he proclaimed: *Yes;*

Whereas what is your life;

Whereas years after they LOOK down from their jets and declare my mother's Abadan block PROBABLY DESTROYED, we walked by the villas, the faces of buildings torn off into dioramas, and recorded it on a hand-held camcorder;

Whereas it could take as long as 16 seconds between the trigger pulled in Las Vegas and the Hellfire missile landing in Mazar-e-Sharif, after which they will ask *Did we hit a child? No. A dog.* they will answer themselves;

Whereas the federal judge at the sentencing hearing said *I want to make sure I pronounce the defendant's name correctly;*

Whereas this lover would pronounce my name and call me *Exquisite* and lay the floor lamp across the floor, softening even the light;

Whereas the lover made my heat rise, rise so that if heat sensors were trained on me, they could read my THERMAL SHADOW through the roof and through the wardrobe;

Whereas *you know we ran into like groups like mass executions. w/ hands tied behind their backs. and everybody shot in the head side by side. its not like seeing a dead body walking to the grocery store here. its not like that. its iraq you know its iraq. its kinda like acceptable to see that there and not – it was kinda like seeing a dead dog or a dead cat lying – ;*

Whereas I thought if he would LOOK at my exquisite face or my father's, he would reconsider;

Whereas *You mean I should be disappeared because of my family name?* and he answered *Yes. That's exactly what I mean,* adding that his wife helped draft the PATRIOT Act;

Whereas the federal judge wanted to be sure he was pronouncing the defendant's name correctly and said he had read all the exhibits, which included the letter I wrote to cast the defendant in a loving light;

Whereas today we celebrate things like his transfer to a detention centre closer to home;

Whereas his son has moved across the country;

Whereas I made nothing happen;

Whereas *ye know not what shall be on the morrow. For what is your life?* It is even a THERMAL SHADOW, it appears so little, and then vanishes from the screen;

Whereas I cannot control my own heat and it can take as long as 16 seconds between the trigger, the Hellfire missile, and *A dog*, they will answer themselves;

Whereas *A dog*, they will say: Now, therefore,

Let it matter what we call a thing.

Let it be the exquisite face for at least 16 seconds.

Let me LOOK at you.

Let me LOOK at you in a light that takes years to get here.

'Look' by Solmaz Sharif, (c) 2016 by Solmaz Sharif, reprinted from *Look* (Graywolf Press, 2016)

Solmaz Sharif

MASTER FILM

my mother around that blue porcelain,
my mother nannying around the boxed grits and just-add-water pantry
of the third richest family in Alabama,
my mother at school on Presbyterian dime and me
on my great grandmother's lap singing
her home, my mother mostly gone
and elsewhere and wondering
about my dad, my baba, driving a cab
in Poughkeepsie, lifting lumber in Rochester, 30 something
and pages of albums killed,
entire rows of classrooms
disappeared, my baba downing Bud Light by the Hudson
and listening to Fast Car, my baba on VHS
interviewed by a friend in New York, his hair
black as mine is now, I'm four and in Alabama, I see him
between odd jobs in different states
and on the video our friend shows baba a picture
of me and asks *how do you feel when you see Solmaz?*
and baba saying *turn the camera off* then
turn off the camera and then
can you please look away I don't want you to see my baba cry

'Master Film' by Solmaz Sharif, (c) 2016 by Solmaz Sharif,
reprinted from *Look* (Graywolf Press, 2016)

Colm Tóibín

BEEKEEPER: PAULA MEEHAN IN THE POET'S CHAIR

In the summer of 1974, Elizabeth Bishop rented a house on the island of North Haven, off the coast of Maine. It was the time of the Nixon impeachment hearings and one of her friends, also staying in the house, kept the television on so that he could follow what was happening. 'If this is "witnessing" history – I'd rather not', Bishop wrote in her journal. She had carried with her the Peterson *Field Guides* to birds and wildflowers and a book on beach pebbles. 'I want now – now that it's too late – to learn the name of *everything*', she noted. But it was not too late.

She began to list in her notebook the wildflowers growing in front of the house – yellow goat's beard, lesser stitchwort, Queen Anne's lace, white clover, ox-eye daisy, red clover, rabbit's foot clover, lobelia, blue-eyed grass, wild radish, creeping bellflower, wild lupine, mullein, purslane, chicory, common morning glory, beach pea, white rosa rugosa, rosa rugosa, fragrant bedstraw, cow or tufted vetch, common St John's wort, eyebright, lesser pyrola. The following year, on her return to the island, she added other names – common evening primrose, bladder campion, harebell. By the summer of 1976, she was staying on the island for a whole two months. She, who had lost so much, had now gained a haven.

During the summer of 1978, when Bishop worked on her poem 'North Haven', her elegy for her friend Robert Lowell, who had died the previous September, she went to her notebooks and her *Field Guide* for ways to withhold the news, from the early stanzas of her own poem, that it was an elegy for her friend. By invoking what she could see and list, she held the world still in her favourite month of the year, invoking also a song from *Love's Labour's Lost* in which Shakespeare uses the phrase, 'paint the meadows with delight':

> This month, our favourite one is full of flowers:
> Buttercups, Red Clover, Purple Vetch,
> Hawkweed still burning, Daisies pied, Eyebright,
> the Fragrant Bedstraw's incandescent stars,
> and more, returned, to paint the meadows with delight.

Thus she used guidebook, notebook, and Shakespeare to make her poem, but she also used her eyes as she moved the flowers from nature to culture, from random, wild presence to highly-wrought use. Soon, in the poem, she invokes birdlife, as she holds her breath before moving the poem's attention to her friend who has died:

> The Goldfinches are back, or others like them,
> and the White-throated Sparrow's five-note song,
> pleading and pleading, brings tears to the eyes.

In her poem 'Death of a Field', in which she dramatizes a battle between nature and culture, between the untamed field and the housing estate, Paula Meehan also invokes birds as abiding presences, whose sounds and rituals are untouched by what is going on below them. She names:

> ... the woodpigeons in the willow
> The finches in what's left of the hawthorn hedge
> And the wagtail in the elder
> Sing on their hungry summer song
>
> The magpies sound like flying castanets

And then she names what will be lost as the field gives way to concrete – scentless mayweed, dandelion, dock, teazel, primrose, thistle, sloe, herb robert, eyebright.

In the following poem ('Not Weeding'), Meehan also names 'Nettle, bramble, shepherd's purse' as versions of the untamed world that do not need to be resolved or assuaged. They flourish where they live; they will persevere without her forgiving or wondering eye.

Her poems set elemental things – sea, sky, bird, tree, weeds – against, or beside, human concerns and complex experiences, almost as Miró placed his elemental shapes and suggestive symbols against the luxury of flat painted colour.

In some of her poems, culture dissolves back into nature often of its own accord, often by the quality of her lyric dreaming, as in 'Number Fifty-One', from the sequence 'Six Sycamores', where the 'red bricks / dream of the clay pit', and 'the iron railings guard the memory of fire', and:

> ... the shutters ache
>
> for the woods, the greeny light, the sap strong
> in bole, in branch, the undergrowth quick
> with life ...

This idea of life, life before certain and uncertain things unmade the world, animates Meehan's poetry and makes her own voice come to life, as though she were operating as a sort of wry, self-contained, fully-alert chorus to a world both tainted and untainted. She wants nature and culture to become aware of each other's fragility and strength.

Elsewhere in her work, when she wishes to cast a spell, her voice is all modesty mixed with carefully controlled power, the cadence rising, ready to soar and heal.

Against this, she is also concerned to people her poems, to mark moments in history, or in her own emotional life, with precision, sympathy, care. Her own gaze as a poet is political, tempered by knowledge and nourished by history, or more likely what has been left out of history, such as:

> the stretcher-bearer, the nurse in white,
> the ones who pick up the pieces, who endure,
> who live at the edge

There is a sense, too, in her work that poetry is a sacred calling, with an ability like no other force in the world to deal with grief and mystery and the space between – the ordinary, the daily, what is remembered and lived through. So that even when she evokes swallows as 'those stitchers of land to sea, those grafters of sky / to the dark earth', she is allowing language this power also, and perhaps even a greater one, with more magic in it and greater force.

Her book, *Imaginary Bonnets with Real Bees in Them* (University College Dublin Press, 2016), transcripts from the three lectures which Meehan delivered when she held the Ireland Chair of Poetry between 2013 and 2016, attempts to offers clues and suggestions about her life, her spirit, her reading and thinking, and her imagination, so that her poems and her poetics can have some slanted light cast upon them.

Her bees in the first lecture live in nature, but Meehan has no trouble with them once she observes how naturally they move into culture. They can be preserved in amber, or can move into language or into memory or into poetry, as though by a natural process.

She wishes to evoke her own haven, the island of Ikaria in the Aegean Sea, one of her own personal or cultural habitats. But she has many other places to recreate and remember, including central Dublin, Finglas, Baldoyle, North America, and Scotland. These *loci* are as important in their contours and what they conjure up for her as the other realms she is capable of inhabiting, the imaginative ones.

Her bears in the second lecture will allow her to ponder on genetics, our origins and the origins of words and myths. They allow her to summon up her own classical education, her early reading, the life she lived when she was beginning. She moves easily, almost stealthily, from precise memory to images and quotations from a well-stocked mind, to moments when she needs to insist on the autonomy of the poem, the pure space that the poem must inhabit if it is to mean something, or do something. When she offers a paraphrase of what her old professor, WB Stanford, thought of poetry, she does not demur. It is clear that this belongs to her too: 'Poetry is not sociology, poetry is not history, is not the sum of the lore and logic it contained, interesting though these things might be; poetry is a way of telling the truth about what it is to be human, a product of the human imagination and a sovereign condition onto itself, coded in measures that are close kin to music and dance.'

Meehan's prose is close in tone to her manner as a poet. She is modest; she allows her voice to remain ordinary and then soar only if the occasion has been hard-won and the new tone is needed. In these lectures, she makes her reading an essential part of her life, as indeed she makes reading her life an essential part of her poetry. There are no false notes, or moments where her confidence has outrun its source. She is always rooted, and then ready to muse and remember, ready to use everything she knows to see through, see into, see beyond.

Words for her are like the body itself, or the city, or anything in nature, or indeed in culture, they are filled with memory that they conceal and release: '*Poetry is memory hungry.*'

In her third lecture, Meehan muses on water and wonders about poetry itself. When she describes living on one of the Shetland Islands in all its wild beauty, she writes: 'I nearly didn't write poetry at all, it seemed like such a puny act compared to the forces of nature shaping and energizing this place. There could be no competition in craft terms. Could I harness some of this power? Was there a lesson in it for my poetry?'

In order to answer this, she calls up a poem by her old teacher, James McAuley, which begins: 'I learn again to take pains / With simple things'.

But in the paragraph before she poses the question, Paula Meehan manages by implication to answer it herself, and indeed reply to the very demands she makes in some of her poems when she, in a visionary moment, wants nature to become a more pure and a less lost space, the soft space from which we come and to where we will return.

In the meantime, there is the untidy nature of the world, its broken culture and cultures, which Meehan evokes in her poems and here in these lectures almost as lovingly, or at least almost as sonorously and energetically, as she does her weeds, her wild flowers, her untouched places.

On another island, Papa Stour, one of the Shetland Islands, she notes: 'There, too, the detritus of western civilisation, colourfully pooling in coves. Plastics. Blue beach bottles, green toilet ducks, plastic bags riding the currents like jellyfish, plastic fish-boxes, the odd boat fender and other items of good honest pruck, an oar, a well-made box, old glass floats, occasionally a beautiful piece of sculpture made by the sea herself.'

Andrew Jamison

ANTI-ACKNOWLEDGEMENTS

I wouldn't like to acknowledge the nobs downstairs
who, despite the many times I've counted to ten
and asked, without expletives, won't turn the bass down.

I am in no way indebted to them
and their Hendrix, and Led Zep phases,
respectively. The time they lit a fire
at 4 a.m. in the backyard has added
nothing to my endeavours. I couldn't
be less grateful to them.

                    My landlord, non-pareil,
deserves no credit whatsoever
for never fitting draft excluders
onto the front door or into the windows,
taking weeks to unblock the sink
and replace the filament in the fan oven.
If it wasn't for his wonderful
negligence so much more of this would have been possible.
He's truly made my life more complicated.

To all my friends who've never bought my book:
words can't convey my scorn.
                                This is for them.

Northern Ireland is a constant source
of homesickness and identity crisis
without which I could imagine a happier life.
Particular thanks to my teachers, and
the village of Crossgar.

X: thanks for the sleepless nights and writer's block;
anytime I go to Portheras Cove
or drive down those corridory Cornish roads
in the unreal light of a vintage summer,
get lost on a walk, or in somebody else's eye
across a table at a Parisian café,
eat scones encased in clotted cream
and (my favourite) raspberry jam,
anytime I taste spice in a Shiraz,
or get a tannin tongue from too much tea
I'll think of you.

Anne Maher

DOWN MEMORY LANE

We met in the early nineteen-seventies,
Elevated by the predominant
Georgian red-brick of No. 6, Ely Place,
Facing Dublin's Hume Street.
We came as young ladies to the Valuation Office
With its elaborately decorated plasterwork,
Following in the footsteps of Sir Richard Griffith,
Pinning our hopes on a pensionable job
In the Civil Service.
Diligent clerical assistants with nimble fingers
Answering phones, stuffing envelopes,
Wading through paperwork.
Peggy Lynch, 'Chief-Sitting-Bull'
Over 'MARKET VALUE'.
We worked with travelling gentlemen
Valuers with *'good suits on their backs'*
Revising land ownership
Mappers with rubbers and rulers
Bent over slender-lined drawings
Profound paper landscapes
Updating old scrunched Ordinance Survey Maps,
Our gaze longingly on the clock
Yearning for a coffee and chat
In O'Donoghue's of Merrion Row.
Returning, we brushed past the paper-keeper:
"Give us a kiss, and a lend of fourpence!"

A.M. Cousins

BEDSIT

Once, the city stood ankle deep in snow
and, in a single bed in Rathmines,
we listened to the joyful news –
sombrely announced at the scrag end
of universal bad tidings –
that schools had closed until further notice.

We walked to Morton's for butter and fruit, sugar and spice.
My cowboy boots let in wet, your work-boots weathered all.

Rolling pastry with a beer bottle
we raised a blizzard of our own.
I filled sweet shortcrust with cloves and apple,
challenged flatland's drag of Vesta curry and cigarettes
as molten caramel flowed,
burned the rented oven.

Proinsias Ó Drisceoil

JAMBOREE

John McDonald, *Tea wi the Abbot: Haiku in Scots* with transcreations in Irish by Gabriel Rosenstock (Onslaught Press, 2016), £10.
Ailbhe Ní Ghearbhuigh, *The Coast Road* (The Gallery Press, 2016), €12.50.

Metre lay at the heart of Gaelic poetry. Changes in metrical practice were invariably reflective of changes in the structure of feeling, and if the modernist poetry which emerged from the mid-twentieth century onwards was less straitjacketed than its antecedents, it was, at its best, conscious of metrical patterns and utilised them pragmatically.

Gabriel Rosenstock's introduction of the Japanese haiku as a serious literary form in poetry in Irish marked a turning away from the kind of nativism synonymous with, say, Daniel Corkery, in favour of the literary cosmopolitanism advocated by Corkery's cultural antagonist, Pádraig de Brún, as articulated in a debate between them in the journal *Humanitas* (1930-1). Irish allowed Rosenstock to go beyond the Anglo-centric provincialism of poetry in English to embrace the culture and poetry of Asia and India, as well as the work of poets in a variety of endangered languages.

The book under review is an instance of the latter, a translation of haikus written in Scots or Lallans, the distinctive form taken by English as it developed in Scotland. (It is not a dialect and is utterly distinct from Scottish Gaelic). While the geographical distance between the Scots language and Irish may not be wide, the cultural chasm is considerable, exacerbated by religious difference and long-established antagonisms between Scots and Gaelic poets. The greatest twentieth-century practitioner of poetry in the language, Hugh MacDiarmid, was neither anti-Irish, anti-Catholic nor anti-Gaelic, but older perceptions have had a long afterlife.

Far from re-running the religious rivalries of the past, McDonald's collection, including the title, is, in many of the poems, driven by aspects of Catholic devotion:

> throu Mass –
> the weet's turnt
> tae snaw

> i lár an Aifrinn –
> d'iompaigh an bháisteach
> ina sneachta

The poet's attitude to the Highlands appears less convinced, however:

hielant veesit –
traikit a'ready
o wattergaws

cuairt ar na garbhchríocha –
bréan den bhogha síne
cheana féin

Succinctness and clarity are renowned features of Scots poetry, and these make that language and the haiku into suitable partners. Rosenstock's translations – or 'transcreations', as he prefers to call them – will be of the greatest assistance to Irish readers in gaining an appreciation of John McDonald's achievement.

Ailbhe Ní Ghearbhuigh's current collection is based on poems previously published in two collections in Irish: *Péacadh* (Coiscéim, 2008) and *Tost agus Allagar* (Coiscéim, 2016). The importance of the present collection lies in the fact that these have now been translated; the latitude given to the translators emphasises their significance. A number of the poems have been translated twice – one of them in separate versions by the same poet – and the invitation to thirteen established poets in English to translate Ní Ghearbhuigh makes the collection a translation jamboree.

Translation is an issue which comes to Irish carrying the burden of Athbheochan na Gaeilge, the language revival, during which the emergence of some gifted poets in Irish from the middle of the last century onwards was offered as evidence of success. Translation was discouraged as it would lessen the incentive to learn the language, and thus, while almost all Scottish Gaelic collections came with translations, poetry collections in Irish were invariably monolingual. In recent years, however, the opportunity to participate in international poetry events and anthologies, as well as a more inclusive attitude towards Irish generally, mean that translation is now commonplace.

Translations do not come without their issues. One of these is the danger that the originals will become secondary to the translations, as has happened with the poetry of Nuala Ní Dhomhnaill in Ireland and Sorley MacLean in Scotland. Secondly, readers without Irish are unlikely to distinguish between versions which seek to closely render the original and those where the poet utilises the themes of the original to produce a new poem. Added to these is the problem of untranslatability, a marked feature of Ní Ghearbhuigh's work. The latter difficulty is at its most apparent in the poem 'Tuathal' ('Anticlockwise'). The word 'tuathal' can mean 'anti-clockwise' or 'left-handed' or 'awkward' or 'error'. In addition, it gives the surname 'Ó Tuathail', which occurs in the poem. Michelle O'Sullivan does her best as translator, but her task is an impossible one. Similarly, 'Deochadh Dorais' faced Peter Fallon with the pun in the poem's title: 'Deochadh' meaning 'immersion', or, as in 'deochadh póg', 'a shower of kisses', or 'deoch an dorais', meaning 'a final drink'. He responds to Ní Ghearbhuigh's pun by giving 'A Parting Kiss' as the poem's title.

The book does not indicate which translators worked directly from the originals and which from cribs. A number of the translators – Michael Coady, Peter Sirr, Paul Muldoon, and David Wheatley, for instance – have an established relationship with Irish; for some others, their versions might best be described as 'imitations' or, indeed, 'transcreations'.

Translators are necessarily critics, interpreting the meaning and significance of the poem and assessing its layers of meaning. Translations which vary considerably from the original may carry the implication that the original is under-realised or, on the other hand, translators may feel that a newly-minted poem on themes derived from the original is the more appropriate response. Vona Groarke's translations are in the latter category: her version of 'Labhraíonn Fear Feasa' (literally, a 'wise man' or 'fortune teller' speaks) is given 'Mindfulness' as its title. Both Groarke ('Morning Song') and Peter Sirr ('Sleeptalk') translate the poem, 'Suanchaint':

> sochraidí
> is tubaistí
> is míle uafás eile.
>
> Feithidí an oilc
> ag dordán
> in ainriail na hoíche ...
>   – AILBHE NÍ GHEARBHUIGH
>
> funerals, disasters
>   and a thousand
>   other terrors.
>
> The insects of evil
> droning
> in the misrule of night ...
>   – PETER SIRR
>
> so a night otherwise funeral-quiet,
> quiet as a threat is quiet, quiet as terror is,
>
> spills, to spite me, my purse of secrets,
> shreds my silence to an insect-buzz ...
>   – VONA GROARKE

Michael Coady only provides one translation, but his translation of 'Cró na Snáthaide' ('Eye of the Needle') manages to achieve reliable translation in a poem which is authentically his own:

> Beag bheann a bhíomar ar an gclog gréine
> a bhí ag áireamh ár laethanta,
> tusa á fháscadh ag scáthanna diamhra.
>
> Too little our heed to the sundial shadowing
> our days and all their counting
> and you being crushed by mysterious shades.

A further insurmountable problem faced here by translators is intertextuality, the extent to which Ní Ghearbhuigh's work invokes other poems in Irish. Predominant among these is the unwritten eighteenth-century Munster lament, 'Caoineadh Airt Uí Laoghaire', whole lines from which are incorporated into certain poems. The influence of twentieth-century Munster poetry is also evident throughout, not least that of Máire Mhac an tSaoi, whose 'Ceathrúintí Mháire Ní Ógáin' provides the framework for 'Ceathrúintí na nÉan' ('Bird Quatrains'), translated by Alan Gillis. Ní Ghearbhuigh's poem uses the anthropomorphic tales of Irish mythology to great effect as the birds of the title takes different forms in a variety of emotional states.

Cultural and social issues animate a number of the poems. In a witty poem on cultural dislocation, 'Filleadh ón Antartach' ('Return from Antarctica'), translated by Billy Ramsell, the returnee refuses his wife's invitation 'to abandon the kitchen / and join her upstairs':

> Is aoibhinn leis
> uaigneas an tsileáin ón sconna.
> Is ceol aige
> srannán an reoiteora ...
>
> He loves the irregular loneliness
> of each tap-drip
> and it's music to him,
> the refrigerator's drone ...

In the poem, 'Rianta' ('Stains'), translated by Medbh McGuckian, the bones of Jean McConville and the Tuam babies make Ireland a landscape of tragic *lieux de Mémoire*:

> Blaoscanna is cnámha beaga,
> beaga, bídeacha.

Rianta balbha ár n-aineolais,
Fianaise ár gcur i gcéill,
Ár gcur faoi cheilt.

Skulls and miniature bones,
dumb reminders of our ignorance,
witness to our makebelieve,
the buried footsteps.

Ní Ghearbhuigh's aesthetic is essentially that of the realist and her genius for succinct narrative is one of her primary gifts as a poet. The poem, 'Bhís dom Thiomáint Cois Farraige' ('The Coast Road'), translated by Peter Fallon, evokes Ian McEwan's powerful novel *On Chesil Beach* (2007), where longing and social mores come into conflict only to issue in inhibition and unfulfilled sexual desire:

Bhís dom thiomáint cois farraige
sa taibhreamh,
ag míniú an cathú a bhí ort,
an fáth nár ligis sinn i gcathú.

Do chuimhníos ansan
ar an mbáisteach bhíoblúil
a fhliuch do choinsias
ar tairseach na dúile.

Dhúisíos le mo dhá chois
i lochán báistí,
clog an tsáipéil
ag áireamh mo bhróin.

Driving by the sea
you were struggling to explain
your scruples, your reason
to lead us not into temptation –
at least you were in my reverie.

And then it all came back to me,
that cloudburst of Biblical
proportions that doused
your conscience on the brink
of my wanting you, your wanting me.

And then, in that rain's shallows,
I came to, up to my ankles in water
and listening to a church's bell
as it knelled and tolled
all my sorrows.

This book places Ailbhe Ní Ghearbhuigh at the core of contemporary poetry in Ireland.

Paul Perry

THE END OF SUMMER

White chrysanthemums
A silent elegy
For summer

I will not have to tell you
When the future has arrived
You will know

Sleeping alone
I heard the cuckoo
It was still dark

I cannot write what I want to write

A golden hare in the garden
Looks up
And is gone

Outside the window
The drip drip of the rain
Onto the child's bicycle seat

I can't sleep I won't

Cutting branches
From the overgrown elm
Which stands between our wall
And theirs

Two scooters lie
In the drive-way
Discarded

I pray for change
I pray for

The end of summer

A siren in the distance
Music on a radio
I try to leave the past behind

Two missed phone-calls
No call back
A stillness

The house silent
And expectant
Waiting for the laughter

And the tears

Putting my sandals away
And looking for socks
School starts tomorrow

Cycling with you on the cross-bar
Up the hill
And cheering me on:
You can do it, you can do it

You are only five
You were only five

Now I am cycling home alone
With no other thought
Than gratitude, than love

A pocket of blue
The trail of a plane

Injured, hurt,
Recovering
I am not going
No bags packed
No passport at the ready
No calls to make
I am staying
I was always staying
I am here
I am here
I am here

Neil Dunne

www.neildavidjames.com

Towers
Screenprint, 77h x 58w cm

The images in this issue are from the exhibition *Young III: A New Generation*
at the SO Fine Art Editions Gallery (**www.sofinearteditions.com**)

Jill Quigley   www.jillquigley.ie

Piggery (Pink)
Photograph, 39h x 60w cm

Sam Le Bas www.lebas.ie

Small Yellow
Spray paint and enamel on aluminium, 63h x 54w cm

Eileen O'Sullivan

Holding onto the Familiar II
Oil on Wood, 40h x 40w cm

www.eileenosullivan.com

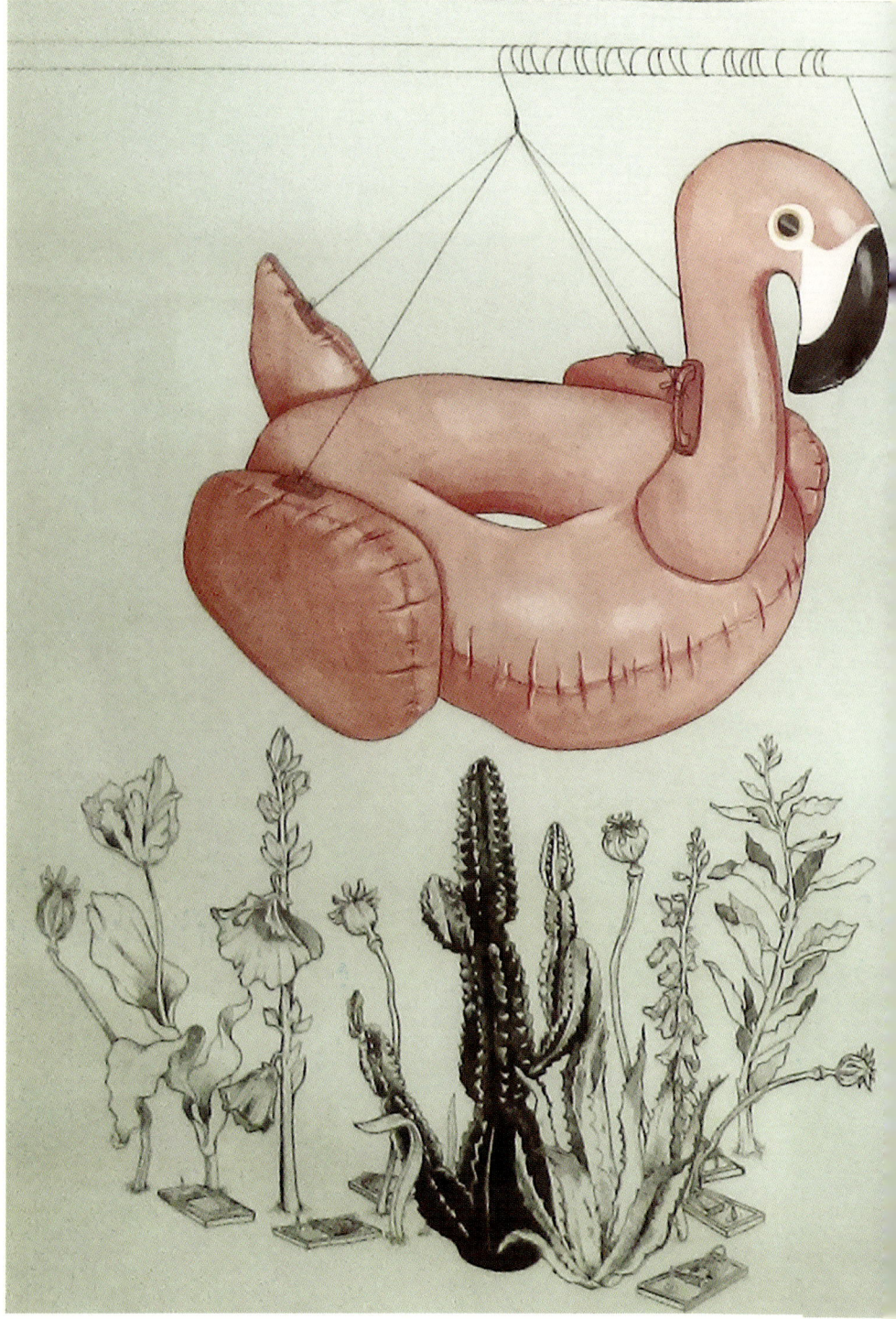

Stephen Lau www.stephenlauart.com

Pseudo Skin
Drawing on paper, 54h x 80w cm

Neil Dunne

www.neildavidjames.com

Parallelism
Screenprint, 77h x 58w cm

John W Sexton

ONE COGNIZANCE

The sedge crowding against the husk
of a rusting motor car has no dream
in its thin many-heads. The car has
no dream either, nor memory. A beetle
skirting the edge of a puddle has the only
cognizance of dream, its pure mind
as smooth as its carapace. In an intake of breath
the beetle is crunched in the mouth of a fox.
The fox steps freely under starlight, the dream
in its mind too, the dream in its mind wide awake.
The stars seep into night, an ichor called starlight.
Starlight penetrates everything, penetrates the dark.
The dark soaks the starlight into itself, draws it in.
The dark soaks in everything, everything penetrates it.
The sedge in its thin many-headed thoughts of nothing
is imbued by every tread of beetle, fox, weasel, mouse,
swift shadows of owls; everything is touched by
and touches everything else. There is one dream,
one sleep, one cognizance wet in the ichor of starlight.

Colette Colfer

MINOTAUR

I am taking him for granted,
this bull-headed man
with his eyes glittery blind.
Look at me, almost death-masked, supine,
my body twisted mawkishly
by his brute thirst and scorching hands.
He is my Asterion, starry guide,
his horns my waxing waning crescents.

I am his labyrinthine maze,
his toreador he will devour.
Look at his grimace over my pubis,
his nostrils overwhelmed by my scent.
He cannot help himself.
And I have cut the thread.
There are trees scratched into the distance.
The sky is blazing.
Fire? Sunset? Dawn?

FROM AN INTERVIEW WITH YVES BONNEFOY, (1923-2016)

In 1987 I was living in Amsterdam, and had been deeply impressed by the poetry of Yves Bonnefoy, and perhaps even more by his prose writings on translation, poetics and art. In Dublin, *Graph* magazine had recently been founded by Michael Cronin, Peter Sirr and Barra Ó Séaghdha. *Graph* was unusual among Irish magazines in that much of its content seemed to be about non English-language writers, reflecting the inclinations of its editors. I knew that Bonnefoy was translating Yeats and would soon be travelling to Ireland. I wrote asking him if he would do an interview for *Graph*. He replied immediately on one of his characteristic rectangular white cards, in his craggy, muscular, handwriting, setting a time, date, and place: the Collège de France in the Latin Quarter, where he held a chair in poetics. I took the train down to Paris, and was a little nervous as I entered those famous and imposing precincts to meet the man I regarded as one of the world's greatest living poets. Bonnefoy was a small man, with a slightly outsized head. Despite his sober business suit, he looked like a man you might meet in a village café anywhere in rural France. He immediately put me at my ease, and was very charming in the sense that he made me feel he and I, a gauche Dubliner with bad French and a few slim volumes to his name, were comrades and co-conspirators in the same great poetic enterprise.

Back in Amsterdam, I sent him a draft of the interview for approval, and soon after received a completely rewritten manuscript. This went back and forth a few times, once being hand delivered to my front door by the French cultural attaché, before Bonnefoy signed off on the final text, which bore little resemblance to the original interview. It appeared in two parts, in issues 4 and 5 of *Graph*, Spring and Autumn 1988. The following extract is from issue 4.

– Michael O'Loughlin

MOL: I find your interest in Yeats puzzling in some ways. One thinks of your strictures on the Symbolists, and how you criticise the Surrealists for preferring 'la roue du paon aux pierres du seuil' ['the peacock's tail to the stones of the threshold']. Your own poetry is very much concerned with a 'true place', always a 'here'. This seems very distant from Yeats's Byzantium.

YB: Yes, I understand that my interest in Yeats's poems, and even in Yeats himself, can seem in contradiction with what I think true for poetry, and particularly my condemnation of the poetics of Symbolism.

But don't you accept the idea that one can love a work of poetry despite its distance from your own? And the more so as there are in it, perhaps, contradictions that make of it the reverse, sometimes, of what it seems to proclaim?

In fact, it is precisely because of my refusal of 'la roue du paon' – of the display of purely aesthetical elements in the Symbolist poem – that I feel very close to Yeats: for, Symbolist as he was, at his beginnings and, in a sense, all his life, he was also capable of understanding the limits, the fundamental delusions that are hidden under what he knew so well. I mean the ideal reconstruction of the world attempted by the Symbolist poem.

Yeats, you know, could never forget that he was a mortal being, deeply involved in the here and now of his existence: and this feeling undermines his most frantic efforts to reach the beauty above. Of course, he was a man of desire, and desire knows how to build its world beyond the grasp of time, in what we can call a dream. But what he was desiring was always a very real object – Maud Gonne, for instance – so that he was summoned back by it to the place, very narrow, and the time, very brief, where and when encountering a Maud Gonne, that is a real, a passing being, was possible.

And as a consequence of this contradiction in his most intimate and constant longings, he wrote these admirable poems of time passing, of desire greater than the dream, of recognition of the absolute value of mortal beings – 'Her Vision in the Woods', 'Among School Children', 'A Bronze Head' and, of course, 'The Circus Animals' Desertion'. Which poet can be more attractive, for those who try to free themselves from the grip of dreams, than this one, who fought so fiercely against his own dreams, and even though he was in fact so often defeated?

> MOL: This summer in Ireland you spoke about Yeats and André Breton, an unusual juxtaposition. Could you say something about this?

YB: The comparison between these two poets is for me a natural consequence of the point of view I am speaking from. For Breton himself, devoted as he was to a dream reconstruction of the self, nevertheless also refused at least part of its usual outcome. In a word, the Symbolist aesthetic reconstruction must borrow its components from the natural world, around and even inside the poet, and the Symbolist poem, its consequence, is therefore quite ambiguous: for, at the very moment it is working out the Idea, the borrowed elements hide this fundamental unreality under the guise of their very concrete, often very sensual, appearance.

And the result is, of course, something very dangerous for a correct assessment of what really is, and matters. But Breton was too impatient of the world in which he had to live to accept borrowing from it. He was attracted by realities that he supposed lay beyond the limits of our perceptions, as these ones usually are in ordinary existence. Therefore the symbolic reconstruction was no longer possible for him, with the consequence that the only thing that he could then experience, in his own life, and express, even indirectly and obscurely, was the pure fact of this expectation of something quite new, of this hope: focusing thus on the one who hopes, that is this man here and now.

Breton as well as Yeats rediscovered the temporal and spatial predicament of the poet, when many others were continuing to substitute the timeless and spaceless aesthetical self-image for the humbler relation that we have day after day with our factual existence. And this was another breakthrough, after so many years of poetical delusion. A truer knowledge of existence was at hand, even though Breton remained the first to forget or repress, through his own sort of dreams, the intuition he had got.

Also, Breton was very much a man of the 'North', as he used to say, and fond of the Celtic civilisations. What he called surreality was in fact part of the Celtic supernatural world of fairies, of furtive apparitions. Had he been aware of Irish myths and legends, he would have been as eager as Yeats to explore them and renew what they say to us.

> MOL: You went to Ireland last August to participate in the Yeats Summer school in Sligo. What does this country mean for you? I notice that you had included it in your *'arrière-pays'* [hinterland] ...

YB: Yes, I too am attracted by the 'North', especially by Ireland. It is not an exclusive attraction as it was for Breton, who never visited Italy or Greece or any other Mediterranean country; and my heart is also in the hills of Tuscany or Arcadia, but the attachment is not lessened by that. Between the two appeals – in a sense two lures – there is in me, a sort of dialectical relationship which I feel constitutive of my own being and present, explicitly or not, in all I write.

What is this relation, this tension? Perhaps the same contradiction which I referred to when speaking of Breton or Yeats. Italy was for me, for a long time, a land where formal perfection, as it can appear in buildings and art, could be so deeply rooted in existing places, among real beings, that we should have to go there to find the absolute at last incarnated in this world. But this belief was a myth, since it asserted the reality of this impossible fusion of form and time; thus Italy was luring me away from what I already knew for the true knowledge – except that time and our own finiteness can only be authentically understood through this sort of prelusive metaphysical delusion. So that this very Italy of my dream (of my reverie of a 'true place') could also be and even truly become, the household of a deeper experience.

But how, among Platonic ideas almost visible in the moving beauty of monuments or paintings, can the epiphany of simple earth take place? It is, I would say, thanks to some small road – by the old chapel in the fields where time has half-destroyed the beautiful images, once the proof that we are exiles from the world of forms – which leads to a ravine, or a bluff, where the clouds part, suddenly allowing the sun to illuminate, for a while, a place here and now, reminiscent of what we were obscurely looking for.

And this road, I daresay, leads thus to Ireland, as the more natural, the easier manifestations of this truth, which both awakened and eluded me in Italy. I like light when it seems to be the transparency, the matterlessnesss of the idea made visible, but I respond to it even more when it is, through what you call a spell of the blue sky – and I don't dislike the ambiguity of the world – the revelation of the beautiful, even absolute, quality of an instant.

This emotion, which I felt very long ago in Brittany, for instance, is the reason why I have since been fascinated by what I was told of Ireland, by what I was perceiving in photographs and also, by what Yeats's poetry was saying: that your country was the farthest shore under the magnificent Western light, which underlines with the colour of blood and youth the glory of the setting shore. And I was attracted all the more because I also know that the hills of Ireland, the worn-out shapes of their summits, the barren slopes of remote valleys disappearing into stones would be for me an image of our bodily conditions, which is so close to matter – I was attracted and so much so in fact, that the call prevented me even so from getting there. It was not that I thought Ireland would be less than my representations of it, it was that the mental image, even when it speaks of time, has an absolute quality, a sort of hidden timelessness which helps us escape this very experience of finiteness that its apparent denial of the realm of eternal forms should have led us to accept.

Returning to the dialectics of the *'arrière-pays'*, which you have evoked: in the very midst of the Irish landscape, now reduced to the status of an image, it was the way back to the Italian chapel, on the walls of which the frescos that fade away also have spells of azure, among the patches of bare stone.

It is easier, in other words, to dream of reality than to live through it, and I preferred to listen to the equally fascinating Irish sounds, since I have been fortunate enough to be given or played, from time to time over many years, records of your old songs, and knew nothing more moving, as well as more beautifully strange, than the melodic line of 'Tis pretty to be in Ballinderry', sung by Mary O'Hara.

Nevertheless I went to Ireland this summer and was not disappointed, even though I was deprived – by lack of time and of a car – of the possibility of going very far along these hillside roads of the hinterland that could lead to truth ... I only caught a glimpse, for instance, of an almost desert region in central Connemara, between the turf and the clouds, where I thought that to stay could be the beginning of a transmutation of the self. But there is also something wherever in Ireland you go, I mean in the eyes of this old man at his door, which is of the nature of the changing sky or the passing leaf. My friend Paul de Man said to me in 1958, when I was asking him the secret of Ireland (where he had travelled the year before), he had replied thoughtfully, after a while: 'Well, this is a country where you can not tell a man from a stone or from a bird', and on the spot I knew that he was right, even if the meaning of the formula was still to be translated into ordinary words.

> MOL: I'd like to ask you particularly about your Yeats translations. What kind of specific problems did you run up against in his poetry, apart from the impossibility of translating it?

YB: Translating Yeats involves some very specific difficulties, of course. To pinpoint only one of them, for I must be brief, I will remind you of the curious fact that there is often in his poems a sort of reasoning. In 'Among School Children', for instance, Yeats has thought, before writing any line, that life cannot fulfil the expectations of a mother. And when he writes the poem he develops this idea, drawing from it some consequences for our possible ethics: his text is a conscious reflection, even if it has to deviate sometimes from its main course because of too many undercurrents in the poet's mind.

The text has, in other words, a sort of conceptual crest, quite visible all along the ridge about the darker slopes that run down both sides. But it also happens that even this crest sometimes has to cross a region of the words that is more cloudy and makes it obscure. And there's the rub, from a translator's point of view, since the reader of the poem can stay as long as he wants with the difficult passage, in order to discover the missing part of the reasoning, and this through a questioning of all the words of the text but without having to dispel the actual phrasing, the actual network of clear and obscure indications. Whereas the translator must either give up a moment of Yeats's thought – and at the cost of breaking what was there covered, not broken – or to make explicit in the translation what was not so in the text for reasons that were perhaps of fundamental importance.

In fact, the explicit thought in a poem is never separated or separable from its undertones among apparently irrational images. It is only an element among many others that have the same right to be and survive, and to follow it in the translation was specifically poetic, by saying much of the explicit and too little, comparatively, of the rest.

What, then, about this hypothetical reconstruction of the missing link which we will draw from the depths of the obscurest passage like a fish perhaps already dying? Both solutions are equally wrong. We cannot accept replacing poetry by conceptual phrasing, and even less to skip over or to imitate without interpretation opaque aggregates of words, as if we were accepting what in fact many translators accept, the belief that a poet writes without trying to say anything. No solution, except this very fact is as such the solution. For, being lost at a crossroads, we, the translators are obliged to resort to our most personal means, that is to enter the task – and even the work – with our own proclivities: a dive which seems sometimes hard to make, but is quite necessary if we want a translation that is more than the dull word-by-word rendering of what originally was freedom and gaiety (as Yeats would have said).

As for me, I decided to be more explicit than the English text, sometimes, but because I saw that I remained very subjective in all my choices of French words. I was already speaking with the poem rather than tracing off the edge of its words, and this fact could make of the over-explicated passage an attempted discussion with Yeats, not a betrayal …

> **MOL:** When I read your translation of 'Among School Children' I was struck, indeed, by these lines in particular:
>
>> Es-tu le tronc, la fleur ou le feuillage?
>> Ô corps que prend le rythme, ô regard, aube,
>> C'est même feu le danseur et la dance.

This is, in effect, a striking image but perhaps not the same one as in the original. I thought immediately of your own lines ...

> L'ange, qui est la terre,
> Va dans chaque buisson et paraître et brûler.

[The angel, who is the earth / Will in every bush appear and burn.]

... and that one could read your translation as Bonnefoy, in this case, as well as Yeats.

YB: Yes, I accept the idea that my translations of Yeats are, in a sense, poems of mine. But I also think that it could not be otherwise. Translating is experiencing something which, if the poem is a great one, that is universal, is an aspect also of our own being, often still unknown to us, still in the process of self-disclosing; and how could we react to these calls made to our life and eventual destiny without being ourselves?

I do not translate a poem into a supposedly common French which is nothing but a myth, but into my own language, my own already begun reenactment of the French language. And this means, of course, that it is very risky to decide to translate a certain poet, for there are differences between human beings which can make the process of fusion, or intimate discussion, quite impossible.

But I also believe that we must not accept to translate a work if we haven't the conviction that there is a sort of kinship between the poet and what we are. I once wrote that the first principle of a theory of translation should be: *Traduisez votre proche* : Translate the poet that you feel closest to you. And later I added that the second (and perhaps only other) principle of the theory should be: *Traduisez-le longtemps*, keep translating him for a long time, possibly all your life, in order to know him more and more intimately. To decide to translate a poet is a very serious act indeed, as much a sacrament as any true marriage or brotherhood; and this decision can seem, therefor, an act of pride when this poet is Yeats or Shakespeare, but I don't think so, since so much of the work has obviously already been done by them. It is, in a sense, a master-and-student relationship, and we need this sort of relation with others, even when we have become more or less ourselves.

As for the foliage and the fire, what I did was simply to stress, I believed, the undercurrent which goes from the *candles* of the seventh stanza in 'Among School Children' to the *midnight oil* of the last one, and above all to the *brightening glance*. There is a flame in these eyes, that are the mirror of the soul of the dancer. But two more problems with this translation, smaller ones: I know that the dancer in Yeats's mind is a female one, there are so many connotations to this word in his work, from the girl dancing in the wind, an image of poetry, to Loie Fuller who, by the way, was wrapped in the wings of a dragon, i.e. fire. But the English word can make us believe this without having to specify that the dancer is not a boy or a man, while the French language must decide, thence, if I say *la danseuse*, this additional and undesirable meaning in my translation: 'don't forget I am not speaking of a man.'

The other problem, still a consequence of what we cannot change in the language that we speak: the *chestnut tree*. As you know, this word also designates what we call in French *le châtaignier* and *le marronnier*, it is the context which makes you able to understand which one of these two different trees is meant by the author of the poem. And in this case it is more likely that Yeats was referring to a *marronnier*, since he speaks of the *blossom*, which is by far less striking in the *châtaignier*. But the *marronnier* is, for us French-speaking readers of Yeats, the beautiful tree of nevertheless quite dull albeit noisy boulevards, near town halls or railway stations. The horizon of the word, the light dust of meaning surrounding it, is society, not nature, no longer the cosmic force that Yeats evokes. I cannot find a good solution ...

Jean Bleakney

STALWART

evokes that Dickensian-sounding
litany of underachievers: navelwort,
non-flowering quillwort, the underwater
awlwort, the milk-less nipplewort,
the floating rootless bladderwort,
the brassier-by-far and toxic ragwort,
but most of all, this double-flowered
soapwort; not 'garden-worthy' as sold
(though not as invasive as feared
at first ... it's been five years) but
tholed nonetheless. A stopgap
between hardy geraniums.

Chelsea Whitton

GRASSHOPPERS

All of the bees have gone or have yet to arrive.

Now the flowers seem suddenly terribly
impotent. There will only be so many now.

Now the sun is so bright is so white it is green.

Our fingers get long in the light.
They get strange and we begin to feel

unwell. We reach hard for each other.
This is the first (and last) day of the world.

I say look. I say smoke.
It is coming way from over there,
way far back behind all those trees.

You say does it have to be smoke?
I say yes and this isn't my fault and I love you.

The world is very old and very innocent.

We lie down.
We lie bellydown in a brown and yellow field.
We lie down in a little quiet.
We say a field is called a quiet, now.

Then we say nothing for a while,
and only comb the quiet grass for grasshoppers.
Some of them are enormous. Some can fly.

They fly away from us, but only far enough to get away.

Is this because they like us, secretly?
Or is it just that they don't want to be alone today?

We half close our eyes.

Now there are clouds.
Now there are many kinds of clouds.
I know the difference. You say there is no difference.

Gerard Smyth

THE HORSE CAME BACK BUT NOT THE RIDER
– On The Lament for Art Ó Laoghaire

The horse came back but not the rider.
There was blood on the saddle
and a cry of lament in the rooms of the house –
a cry they heard in the next parish,
in Macroom and *The Gearagh* –
the sound of loss in a dying language.

The horse came back but not the rider
who in his haste forgot that the long grass
could hide a sorrow-maker –
the one whose high noon bullet would pass
through the heart of the oral tradition,
killing the horseman but not the horse

that galloped back to the stable yard
and Eileen waiting, the Queen of Keening
whose youthful beauty left no trace
in the days of her long siesta,
when every dream was a playback of the scene
when the horse came back but not the rider.

Theo Dorgan

JOHN MONTAGUE: THE INFLUENCE OF ANXIETY

It is, I think, a dangerous thing for a young poet to place what burgeoning gift they might have under the protective benevolence of an older poet. There are, of course, instances of such benevolence having wholly positive effect, the seeking and giving of wise and unselfish guidance, best of all disinterested guidance, proving out to the mutual benefit of both teacher and apprentice. Such instances are rare. Young poets are so vulnerable: if there is any chance that they will stay the course, then their beginnings will likely be marked by doubt, uncertainty, a resigned conviction that what they are writing does not deserve the light of day, will bring them only shame; if, on the other hand, they have already begun to swagger, to pronounce and pontificate, there is a very good chance that in time they will find a more congenial path for the ego to express itself, letting poetry fall away. The first kind, the doubters we might call them, need to find a way to summon and build on some kind of stubborn confidence, the second need trimming, severity of response, some opening of the affective response into humility. The well-meaning older poet, presented with a clutch of tyros in a teaching environment, has some difficult decisions to make in terms of building relationships with, typically, a handful of varying personalities: in the first place, he or she has to decide on the general level of engagement they are prepared to offer; in the second place, they will have to work out the balance between closeness and distance warranted in each individual case; thirdly, he or she will need, or so it certainly seems to me, to have a lively awareness of the dangers inherent in cultivating acolytes.

For the senior poet, an acolyte may be a temporary balm to momentary hurts, but with a sad inevitability the acolyte will one day come to resent a relationship founded essentially on dependence. Almost certainly, sooner or later, the son/daughter will be moved to kill off the mother/father, to the general unhappiness of all.

Old enough now to have seen these dynamics from both ends of the spectrum, I find it difficult to examine, as I have been invited to do here, what the nature was of John Montague's influence on me as a young poet – I was, I see now, as rebellious and mule-headed as I was riven by doubt, as determined to go my own sweet way as I was, all unaware, well placed to benefit from instruction and sound advice. Not, in any case, acolyte material. I was prepared to befriend Montague with the careless offhandedness of the young and foolish, and I was happy to be befriended by him, but I had no interest at all in feeding his ego, which was not inconsiderable, and still less was I in search of a father figure – in the following decades I would be obliged to pull him up very short indeed when he would claim literary paternity in my work. Nonetheless, I realize now that I could have benefited more from his presence in Cork had I been less independent, and had he been more disposed to understand, perhaps forgive, my combative insecurity, and his own.

John came to teach in University College Cork in 1972, when I had begun a degree in English and Philosophy. All I had read of him was *Tides*, which I thought a good book of love poems, and a handful of reviews he had contributed to the fortnightly *Hibernia*. I knew he had come to UCC at the instigation of Sean Lucy, Professor in the English Department and a good friend to poets, and I also knew, I don't remember how, that Lucy had been prompted by Seán Ó Riada to create the post of Assistant Lecturer for Montague. He came with an exotic pedigree, a reputation as a cosmopolitan, and with a faint, agreeable, scent of sulphur attached. This last was due, I think, to those already published sections of *The Rough Field* that had promised a more engaged relationship with the emerging troubles than had appeared, thus far, in Heaney – of whom we were very aware and, for obscure reasons, already proud.

It was a small company of apprentice poets that Montague found waiting for him in UCC. The luminous Irish-language cohort we knew as the INNTI poets were already completing their studies, and there was a sense, in the English Department certainly, that the next wave would be ours. Maurice Riordan, Greg O'Donoghue and Pat Crotty were a year ahead of me, O'Donoghue supercilious and faintly patronizing, Riordan friendly but somewhat remote, Crotty already possessed of an unparalleled memory for verse of all kinds and epochs.

In my own year, Seán Dunne from Waterford, like myself the son of a factory worker, was already very much under the influence of Douglas Dunn and politically reddish and vocal, while Thomas McCarthy, steady, already very well-read, adventurous and a gifted craftsman, was in many ways the most mature of our slowly expanding circle. In time that circle would include the excitable and ebullient Greg Delanty, the ever-amiable and always shrewd and incisive Gerry Murphy, and Liam de Bhál who would soon become William Wall, for reasons I never quite understood.

A motley crew if ever there was one, yet Montague took us seriously enough to open the doors to us of the house he and Evelyn had taken in Grattan Hill. We were made welcome in that house, made feel at home.

If the bills and mundane correspondence ended up on the kitchen table, while reviews, letters of invitation and other insignia of the advanced literary life were left lying about on the hall table, we might have seen the small vanity of it, but we sensed, or certainly Tom and myself sensed, that this was John's way of signalling to us that there was a literary world beyond the provincial bounds of our damp and foggy city, that he belonged out there, and that we, too, however peripherally, had an engagement with that wider world through our common, if uneven, commitment to the craft.

His presence, or the fact of his presence, in that world of literature mattered a great deal to John. He was pleased to let us know of his acquaintances and friendships, with Gary Snyder, for instance, with Robert Duncan, Claude Esteban, André Frénaud, and many others with whose names, if not always whose work, we were or might be familiar. Even then, for I often discussed it with McCarthy, it was evident that Montague was anxious, somehow, about the nature and future security of his reputation. He desired a reputation, was even then concerned with how his work was received, what place in the pantheon posterity would assign to him. I was uneasy about this concern for reputation, already sure that the only thing that truly mattered was the poem, that all else was dross and a dangerous bother. This, of course, was all of a piece with my modish disdain for money, position and status, but all the same I was clear on this, that the only specific against both destructive vanity and disappointment was a ruthless concentration on the poem, the poem itself and the poem only. I might have struggled then to express my discomfort with that aspect of John's ambition, but Tom summed it up perfectly for us in his early poem 'Daedalus, the Maker', when he said, in effect, that the artist's sole business, indeed highest duty, was 'to lay art anonymously at earth's altar'. I never discussed the phrase with John, but I am sure he would have found it baffling, or even naïve, just as I am sure he would have suspected that Tom didn't really mean it but, then as now, Tom only ever says what he means.

That John was frequently disappointed in his vanity, I could see clearly, and I was influenced by what I saw, confirmed in my seed-suspicion that anxiety about reputation could be destructive of the life and of the work. Nobody who publishes work can or should be indifferent to its reception, to the flush of affirmation experienced when a review or a reference shows that somebody, somewhere, has read the poem you hoped you had written. Praise is good for soma and psyche, but only if it is right praise, earned by the work and the work only. If only by indirection, I learned that first by studying how John endeavoured to place himself in the world's favour, and seeing how little good he had of the effort, how vulnerable he left himself to the vicious and mean-minded.

I admired John's poems enormously, and I still do; he was a master craftsman, had an uncannily accurate ear for syllabics, for the placement of sounds in the overall tonality of a poem, and he covered a great deal of ground in his themes and his topics – he was, for instance, ecologically conscious well in advance of the times, his handling of tribal memory and the uneasy passage of pain through politics in our time was both subtle and moving, and he had the true lyric gift. I learned from John that the lyric is far more resourceful and protean a form than was then being widely granted. He was, as I learned to be, a great admirer of the brave and capacious American lyric with its broad compass – it was through John, for example, that I first encountered Galway Kinnell, in the form of *The Book of Nightmares*, a touchstone book for me.

Montague has often been praised as a love poet, with some justification, but I thought then, and I think now, that he had the same trouble in writing love poems that Yeats sometimes had: for all that he saw himself, quite genuinely, as a lover, Montague often seems to write *of* women as emblems or recipients of his gift of attention, rather than *to* women as independent persons, by which I mean that in some strange sense he experienced love as a kind of conflicted affliction, was therefore anxious about women and their responses to him. I think that the only time we were truly angry with each other was on a misty spring afternoon, on high stools in Paddy Barry's bar on MacCurtain Street. He had been reading some poems of mine, now entirely and justly forgotten, and when he came to the closing line in one, 'Love, the practice of care towards the beloved', he just exploded, began to rave at and berate me, red-faced, scornful, genuinely raging. I was to understand that I knew nothing of love, that this was not love, and so on. And so on. I know that I called him some pretty names in the ensuing row, but even as I raged back at him I was wondering what raw nerve I had touched, what it was about women as persons, or men as caring in love, that had set him off. To be clear and fair, then and later I would see ample evidence of his capacity to be tender and empathetic; nevertheless, that memory endures.

Of course our friendship, for it had by then become a friendship, survived that row, as it would survive many lesser rows thereafter, but I saw that there was a gulf fixed between his world and mine.

One further argument we had is not, perhaps, unrelated to this, although it would come decades later. John firmly believed that the irreparable wound caused by being, as he saw and felt it, abandoned by his mother at the age of four was the truest and deepest source of his poetic gift. I accused him once, in the course of a long evening into night, of deliberately cultivating that wound, which was insensitive of me but not untrue, and he denied it, which was foolish of him, perhaps, and certainly unconvincing. I ask pardon of his ghost for any further anguish I might have caused him then, in the mistaken belief that I might somehow persuade him to alleviate his pain by letting go of it; I would have done better to keep my mouth shut. That said, I learned from John, by indirection, long after our bruising exchange, that the ceaseless revisiting of a primal experience is more likely to prove a closing down than an opening up. Cavafy's beautiful poem, 'The God Abandons Antony', teaches us that if a time should come in a poet's life when it seems as if the gift may be withdrawn, or even that it *has* been withdrawn, one should at all costs maintain a stoic and respectful dignified silence. A gift, after all, only matters or means when it is freely given, not when it is gained by stratagem or guile.

There are, or can be, beneficial manifestations of anxiety, as every craftworker knows. Not all forms of anxiety are destructive. John was forever searching for poems, forever working and reworking poems, trying out phrases, rhythms – there is no doubt but that poetry, the making of poems, was at the centre of his life. I never borrowed a book from him without finding, in that crabbed minuscule hand, notes and observations in the margins, sometimes between lines, and often, in the blank pages at the back, a verse or more of something I might long after recognize in a finished poem. He was, if I might put it like this, anxious for poems, always on the *qui vive*, antennae quivering. This, too, was an influence. I was hungry for every kind of sensation in those days, a creature of appetite, drawn most easily to what was vivid and immediate. From John, slowly, I began to learn that one must be prepared, when the first intimation strikes or dawns, to retreat into silence, to concentrate the attention on the poem that might be announcing itself. Too, he was ever-anxious to ensure that a poem was as right in itself as craft could make it, hence the ceaseless working and reworking in the service of the poem. I think that he found in Robert Graves affirmation of his own sense that a poem somehow pre-existed its appearance on the page or in the mind's eye, that the poet's business was to work back or out or through to the ur-poem, accepting that full convergence between the poem-in-itself and the poem as achieved by craft could never, quite, be fully accomplished. He thought it his duty, in the light of this, to do his damnedest by means of unremitting work to make the artefact in words, the thing on the page, as close as possible to a perfect simulacrum of the poem in its imagined, intuited, Platonic perfection. This anxious desire to be true to the poem was what drove his unremitting devotion to craft, and to varying degrees we, his student-friends, acquired a like devotion.

It was from Robert Duncan, he told me once, that he learned the importance of shaping a collection of poems into an organized whole. He would agonize for a long time about where a particular poem would work best in relation to other poems, not just in terms of narrative coherence or sequence but in terms of chimes and echoes of mood, colour, sound and other orchestral elements.

So, craft, duty, fidelity to the self-intending poem, orchestration of effects, the managing of poems into shaped and intended books, a ceaseless learning from the successes and failures in poems by other hands, all these things I learned first, in varying degrees, by being in John's company, through the osmosis that operates in the penumbra of companionship. With Tom especially, with those others to varying degrees and in different ways, I felt I had signed on for the long haul in serious company – but John was our first Great Companion, and for all the storms and turbulence that would mark the years that followed, for all the ebb and flow of affection and recrimination, of charge, counter-charge and forgiveness that marked our relationships with him, we none of us, ever, doubted or slighted his unswerving faith in the truths of poetry.

When after a long anabasis in the world, Greg O'Donoghue came home in the 1990s, reborn it seemed to me as the kind of burning Saint one finds in the Ikons of Kiev, I would seek him out whenever I, in my turn, should be in Cork. Inevitably, at the round table in The Long Valley, the conversation would turn to Montague, his doings and whereabouts, his poems in the short perspective and the long. Life had burned out of us those first fine certainties, the early anxieties, the airy careless dismissiveness of the young, and we could see for and in ourselves, the pain that a man or woman can endure and cause, the great difficulty of finding a way to give honest witness in this life. It took us a long time to puzzle out the hidden, thankful, humility in John, that note of grace which, once we had found it, we could trace in so many of the great poems. It took us a long time to see, what had been hidden in plain sight, that so many, so very many of the poems have in them the music of gratitude. Not least, in poem after poem, gratitude for the gift of the very poem itself.

Theo Dorgan

GOING HOME
   i.m. Manos Kazakopoulos

Come, Kapetan, we've a fair wind for Ikaria,
a sound boat and a steady crew – you know them well,
friends of your youth, good companions all.

Give me your hand and step aboard; the night
is coming on, we've a star or two to steer by,
come sit here by the helm and take your ease.

South-east to clear the roads then round to the north –
how many times have we made this course
on good days and bad, all these long years?

Dear friend, just think of it, so many journeys,
such treasure of memory stored in our bones!
How fortunate we have been in our wanderings

over the broad sea, the fruitful, fragrant earth –
and what have we learned? That all voyages
have a beginning and an end. Just so.

They will be lighting the lamps in Agios Kirikos,
setting the tables, gathering to the tavernas,
an eye to the harbour entrance, the incoming craft –

a fine welcome they'll have for you, home at last
to a berth under the Atheras, under the olives.
Friend, we are at your service, give the command.

Aifric Mac Aodha

GÓ

Aithnítear nach leor seo, nach leor taobh na fothana ná faisnéis na heachtra, nach leor an siar is aniar a luíonn le hainm is fíor, roimh oscailt súl na maidine. Aithnítear nach leor seo.

Tá cúig bliana déag ann ó d'éag m'athair, fear a dúirt faoi anáil an mhoirfín dó, *Of all the bishops, I speak the best Latin*. Tá a fhios agam nach leor seo. Ach mo mhilleadh féin i m'aonar – an focal bearrtha – níl ionam fós imeacht uathu.

Leor is leorghníomh, ní hionann – aithním, a chuid, nach leor seo.

*

Fágann an bhearna
idir seo is sin
nach ceadmhach
a bhfuil caite

a ligean le neach –
an focal féin, neach,
ní ceadmhach
é a ligean isteach.

Ní ceadmhach
fiú, ceadmhach.
Tagann siad, an fhainic
is an oscailt faoi seach.

*

Cé leis an imirt,
an t-athrú uabhair?
Éislinn gan chosaint
an éist linn dúchais.

Tugtar suas don riadaire,
mámh is drámh na teanga,
an radaire a thuigeann
– ar nós an rince –

Aifric Mac Aodha

LIED

It's well-known this isn't enough, the word of comfort or bare bones
of the thing won't cut it, the to and fro that comes with a name,
before you open your eyes in the morning, won't do. It's well-known.

Fifteen years ago my father died, a man who said under the influence
of morphine, 'Of all the bishops, I speak the best Latin'. I know it
won't do. But the skeleton of the language – that solitary self-undoing
– I still can't see a way out.

A sufficiency and a sufficing deed, they're not the same thing. I
recognize it, love, it won't do.

*

The gap between
this and that means
it's best not breathe
a word to a soul.

Best forbid it –
the very word 'soul',
best not let
the word in at all.

Don't allow
'allowed', even.
They'll come, your chance
and your warning, in turn.

*

Who owns the game,
the upending of pride?
The unguarded tongue needs
someone to come to its aid.

Give in to the Elder,
that ace and deuce,
the ranter who gets it,
when the dance-shoes go on –

go bhfuil na seanchéimeanna
imithe i léig orainn,
nach athbhríoch don athbhrí
ach a gcaitear siar ró-éasca.

*

Ar an riadaire, óltar deoch,
ach géilltear fós don réice.

Fear na gceirníní,
airíonn ag teacht í,
dreach Monroe
ar a sála daite.

Tá, ar a ghob aige,
an freagra sciobtha,
gur nua ag Marilyn dul
ag breathnú suas sciorta.

Cé d'iarrfadh
athrú ceoil air,
an tsúil le goimh,
an chos i dtaca?

*– Lena cheart a thabhairt dó,
an insíonn seisean dise céard a ólas sí?*

*

Cé leis an imirt,
An t-athrú uabhair?
Éislinn gan chosaint
an éist linn nua.

Cuireadh chun dinnéir,
is an dá lámh dúnta –
promhadh, ní priocadh
a d'ordaigh an nuachar.

Ná ní gaisce a gcáineadh,
lánúin na fáilte,
an t-oráiste craorag
á chaitheamh eatarthu.

that nothing remains
to salvage our failure
but all the old steps
we've thrown off the dance-floor.

*

Have a drink on the ranter –
but know the lad's top dog.

From his booth the DJ reels
her in with his eyes, the spit
of Monroe in
her dayglo heels.

The snappy retort
on his lips: not what
Marilyn's known for,
looking up skirts.

With a canny eye
but stony-faced,
who'd ask this guy
for a special request?

*– To give him his due,
the DJ doesn't tell her what to drink.*

*

Who owns the game,
the upending of pride?
Listen to us, tone-deaf,
but trying to get you onside.

Housebound without
home-care for your hang-ups:
high time to be shot of him,
and with him your handcuffs.

Though there's nothing heroic
in doing down
the lovely couple
with their purple oranges.

Ise ag maíomh
as a chniotáil seisean,
eisean ag maíomh
as a déantús miotail.

★

Ní foláir ligean leis,
mar bhrú ar an doicheall –
cróilí gan tindeáil
a theastaigh sa deireadh.

Drochrath ar an altra,
í ag fústráil faoin mbord,
an goile fánach
is an lón os a chomhair.

Tabhair meilte
ar na blianta a lean,
ar an gcuthach ceilte
a d'éirigh ina bean.

★

Is aithnítear arís nach leor seo, nach leor taobh na fothana ná faisnéis
na heachtra, nach leor an siar is aniar a luíonn le hainm is fíor, faoi
sholas dearg óstáin. Aithnítear nach leor seo.

Uamanna is lingeáin chuilce an chéad shraith, tá ráillí an Luas á gcur
síos – cuain an earc luachra, nár rugadh is nár saolaíodh.

Tá a fhios agam é, a chuid – ní leor seo.

★

Ná ní leor, ach oiread,
an chríoch is a háiteamh
nach dtagann den chuairt
ach beannú na cnáimhe.

An bhfuilim fós
le tarraingt air,
an leithscéal sin
gan dealramh?

Herself all talk about
his knitting tea-cosies,
himself boasting
about her intricacies.

*

Best stop pushing
on a closed door;
keep out the crowd that
has her driven spare.

Bad cess to the nurse
spraying his table,
his appetite gone
and his lunch waiting.

Grind down to nothing
the years still to come,
the hidden fury that's grown
into a woman.

*

And have it recognized, again, that this won't suffice, erring on neither the side of a word to the wise or telling it straight, nor a drawn-out back-and-forth over a tavern glass.

Stitches and bedsprings are first – The Luas rails are being laid. The young of newts not born, not given birth to.

I know it well, my love – this won't do.

*

What's it still worth
to you, trips to the boneyard
your father's cancer-riddled
body became when laid in earth?

Am I still writing
cheques on it now,
that rickety old
excuse?

Och, ní galar aon
duine amháin é,
is galair ann
atá níos measa.

*

Ní leomhtar guth fir a rá
ach a ghuth féin, labhair fireann –
imeoidh seo, dúirt sé,
é seo, ní mhairfidh.

Áitím, ann sin,
gur shanntaíos
fear nár liom féin,
nárbh é a leath a leath de.

Ní cheadaítear guth mná a rá,
ach guth m'óige, d'fhreagair é –
a bhfuil tuillte agam cheana, gheobhaidh,
    a bhfuil curtha agam, bainfidh.

Tsk, but it's no one's
doom and theirs alone,
this one life in common
we have to lose.

*

It shouldn't have been, but it was
a man's voice holding forth –
this too will pass,
he said; it's not forever.

And, I confess, I coveted
a man not mine, and who
he was was neither
all nor half of it.

It shouldn't have been but was
a woman spelling it out to the man –
it's yours to keep, what you have, you hold,
    and what I've sown, I'll reap.

                              – translated by **David Wheatley**

Richard W Halperin

BY A FIRESIDE, DECEMBER

I listen to the lute music of John Dowland.
Seven tears, lachrimae, written in exile.
I read the poetry of Teri Murray, Irish,
Not in exile, except as all artists are in exile
From childhood on. Her strings: gut, and certainty.
Her poems hang in air, shining things.
To younger poets, I would recommend:
Shame. Then, respect for what is left.
Then, language: words well fitted together,
As in the carvings of another Irish artist,
Benedict Tutty. There is no England
Or Ireland in such things. There is the fashioning
Out of oneself an individual colour,
As instantly recognizable as a chick to
Its mother. Happiness cannot produce this,
Nor can tragedy, although both are necessary.
Lachrimae.

Thomas Dillon Redshaw

TURN AGAIN

Thomas McCarthy, *Pandemonium* (Carcanet Press, 2016), £9.99.
Mary O'Malley, *Playing the Octopus* (Carcanet Press, 2016), £9.99.

Taking the backward look, *Poetry Ireland Review*'s readers cannot help but note the sudden flush and achievement of poets born in the 1950s who began to claim their audiences in the late 1980s and early 1990s – among them Thomas McCarthy and Mary O'Malley, both born in 1954. In different ways, their new collections from Carcanet Press hint that their poetry will take a new turn. O'Malley came in to Ireland's writing life through Jessie Lendennie's Salmon Poetry, and then joined Eavan Boland and Paula Meehan in *Three Poets from Ireland* from Michael Schmidt's Carcanet, itself a product of the teeming 1970s. McCarthy began his writing life in the enclosed gardens of Waterford and then entered the Cork City library service. First associated with Liam Miller's Dolmen Press and with the Triskel poets of Cork in the nimbus of Patrick Galvin and John Montague, McCarthy gave most of his eight collections – including his early 'best seller' *The Sorrow Garden* (1981) – to Peter Jay's remarkable Anvil Press in London, whose titles Carcanet rescued in 2016.

There's an economy and a sociology here that literary historians of twentieth-century Ireland will ponder. But what, on leave from the press of Irish life since 2008, the careful Irish writer might note from her residency at the Irish College in Paris, or his perch in Prague or Aberdeen, is a minatory sensation in both McCarthy's *Pandemonium* and O'Malley's *Playing the Octopus*. Sensible and even sought for in both collections is the immanence of changes – a 'late style', even – in the coming composure and performance of their poetry. In the over-taught aftermath of Late Yeats and Late Yeats, this is a change-up that some Irish poets have handled well – as does Kinsella and as did Heaney.

Registering this immanence on almost every page, McCarthy's *Pandemonium* begins with a farewell – an elegant verse letter to the late Dennis O'Driscoll – and ends with a farewell darkly echoing the title poem of *The Non-Aligned Story Teller* (1984). Indeed, by allusion and verbal echo, *Pandemonium* looks back from the dismays of the present to the histories, legends, and personal myths that McCarthy's inventiveness displayed so tellingly in his past collections – small-town Fianna Fáil Ireland, mercantile Cork, the fading Anglo-Ireland of the Fitzgeralds and the Keanes. McCarthy remembers a day digging for Mrs Cockburn in 'Agapanthus':

> She had just published a good book, her autobiography
> That kept her friends straight and her enemies crooked,

> But as if the world needed to show a woman of quality
> What indifference meant, or how landlords could still be shit,
> The letter was not an offer for film rights but a notice to quit.

Pandemonium offers up good-byes and safe-homes to an Ireland that McCarthy has discovered so surprisingly over the past four decades. And there is sustenance for both poet and reader in letting these kindly fictions find their own afterlives. A sweetness remains in poems like 'Social Class in West Waterford' or 'A Sound in the Woods' and especially 'Largesse', that lean back one last time into the domain of *The Sorrow Garden* (1981).

One of McCarthy's vintage tropes is, of course, the garden, and it comes to the fore just at the close of *Pandemonium* – like the bitter sweet moral in Voltaire's *Candide*, or the plangent choral Bernstein made of it. In 'Digging in December', a wonderful meditation on effort and exasperation, he stands at the bottom slope of his Montenotte plot 'working this late in the year' like all poets 'and full of a hopeless guilt' – working to set the garden right, to put the pear tree it its place. All that last-minute rage for order can come from anger, from dismay at the costs that Ireland paid in the lapse after the collapse of 2008. No wonder John Martin's painting *Pandemonium* (1825) appears on the cover: the Sumerian pile of Beelzebub and Brothers LLC looking oddly like the Houses of Parliament at Westminster. Malton's view of Leinster House or a glossy of flag-draped offices in Brussels would not do. No wonder, alas, that an unroofed Famine cottage rests reconstructed in United Nations Plaza in Manhattan. 'Slow Food', McCarthy's brave poem on the displacement theme, is a wonder of perspective and inversing tone:

> ... All of this complete snobbery of the gut, might bear down
>
> Upon one dying child. Here is my Euro, child. Here is
> The olive oil and the stuffed artichoke. Here is the conscience
> And the conscience money. They stole my land too ...

McCarthy tempers *Pandemonium*'s themes with a teasing delight in way-out words, as did Father Prout way back when (or Father Dineen in Irish): 'orpiment,' 'eigentone,' 'susurrant'. He tempers them by finding lines – lyric, conversational, sometimes recalling the ease of Derek Mahon – and unaccustomed forms, as in a set of prose poems in the centre of the book. But what every reader will note almost from the start is a new ground metaphor in McCarthy's poems here – the image of the tide-washed, broad and sandy beach peopled by Ireland's retinue of sand-pipers and oystercatchers. 'At Ink Level, The Sea' gives one of many instances: 'So many oyster-catchers thread the surf ...' Here we have the summer sands near Ballyferriter or the late-Autumn wash on Ardmore strand. McCarthy offers this family of images – birds, sand, tide – throughout *Pandemonium* as if to pose it now not so much as the final but more as the first answer. As a metaphor for living, this has its risks. As a metaphor for writing, though it proposes an opening to the saving lift of the lyric.

As any reader's pencil ticks against McCarthy's lengthening lines will attest, *Pandemonium* edges up to this immanence so repeatedly that it is a worthwhile risk to read Mary O'Malley's *Playing the Octopus* – a wry allusion to the trials of wrestling a tune out of the uilleann pipes – with immanence in mind as well. O'Malley and McCarthy share a generation, share in remaking Ireland's poetry, and share a Continental *nostalgie de la fin*. One similarity uncloaks others. The trope of her title and her collection's cover image – the shape-shifting, self-camouflaging, self-cloaking grey octopus – startles. Like McCarthy with his *hortus closus*, O'Malley resorts to the long lineage of English verse when she starts her poems out with Milton, whose time was bad for Ireland. O'Malley's other humours – Iberian, Gaelic, Continental, American – counter the unframed moral of her line from *Paradise Lost*: 'Long is the way and hard, that out of Hell leads up to light' (II, l. 433). Satan says this to the parliament of devils in Pandemonium. Later, O'Malley's epigraphs offer TS Eliot, Dante, Hartnett, a nameless *New York Times* science reporter. Likewise, her suites of translations from Seán Ó Ríordáin and Frederico Garcia Lorca work as epigraphs. *Playing the Octopus* has a four-fold sequence: old traditions surfacing in daily life; west country nature shedding it protective colours; the edge of America …; and then to the invisibilia of language and its particulars. O'Malley offers a squaring up of worldly experience. There's immanence posed there because her art addresses that 'convex' over Pandemonium – that vault behind which our Earth and God's Heaven wait.

Addressed to Sligo's Dermot Healy, O'Malley's stunning, comical riff on the finding of her very own graven idol – 'The Angel of Camden Street' – opens *Playing the Octopus*. By ending that humoresque with 'And the Blessed Virgin looks up and asks, / "Now who in the Lord is that?"' O'Malley lets the language of local incident shimmer with the remains of Marian Catholicity. Likewise, having worked squarely around to 'A Lift,' an accomplished Irish elegy to Healy, the reader discovers that O'Malley's repeated phrase 'a shower of particles' – one repeated from the Book of Einstein – has changed into a an immaculate vision untouched by the fact that 'The world goes on as wicked as before, or worse / Whatever history says.' That change of hue and shade appears as good as a rainbow through Healy's rain-spattered windscreen as he drives up the pass to Enniskillen headed to Derry:

> And always the clouds parted and anything, statues
> Soho strippers, homeless boys, a sinking cruise ship

> Could appear there, out of nothing, like a flock
> Of Maybirds because that's also how life is. Pure magic.

O'Malley's habits of line and lexicon in *Playing the Octopus* feel freer than McCarthy's craft in *Pandemonium*, but they are not less purposeful. At the start, O'Malley takes the reader aback with the Puritan precision of 'Scarce' after treating – in 'Show Time' – a midnight cloudscape as if it were marine painter's view of Galway Bay whitecaps, and as if that were the parade at the Galway Races, and all along suggesting they are our *cauchemars*. On the second side of O'Malley's squaring, plain-spoken tree and animal poems modulate into a riff on the legend of Suibhne Geilt. On the west side of her squaring come poems placed mostly on the American East Coast. They take up the circumstances of immigration, language, of writing in exile, of New York City and Philadelphia – all closing, as the book itself does not, in a preparatory forgetting. The signal, highly audacious poem here is 'Forgotten': 'No one remembers / The bad thief's mother. Gestas – full of anger.' Again, ordinary themes give way to immanence. North on the squaring – Healy's Sligo, Leitrim, and Donegal – come the translations, the changes, *na h-aistriúcháin* and then a quartet of fine closing poems: 'Subtraction', 'All Souls', 'At Cré na Cille', and 'A Lift'.

Playing the Octopus and *Pandemonium* are collections admirable both in detail and through-composed conception. Both books hazard in full career each poet's perspective on the place of poetry in an Ireland made morally and ethically ordinary by the passing of the 'Troubles' in the North and the consequent evaporation of cultural certainties in the Republic. The late passings of the poets – of O'Driscoll, of Heaney, and now of Montague – bring forward hopes and worries that bother and elate both poets. In 'Occupation', O'Malley joins Satan's party and goes back to tropes of language – Gaeilge agus Béarla – favoured by Montague and Ó Dhomhnaill: 'Our tongues / Blunt like knives in drawers / Too long unused.' There's a teasing savagery in the glint, there, of her last line: 'we only need / To win once, like freedom fighters / With a song that blows the house down / Or up, if that is your tune.' More mildly McCarthy takes up with his contemporaries while on the strand at Ballyferriter, gazing out at the slick sand and shorebirds and pulling together rhymes for a Mahonesque verse review of John F Deane, John Goodby, and Peter McDonald. And McCarthy gives us three roles for the Irish poet: enfolding 'Both God and eight-hand reels in poetic dress'; writing 'With the aplomb of a man in a cage'; and recalling 'the dead / Or the gone, or the going. With such love…' All three roles help us prepare for what may come.

Eithne Hand

HARD CHAW

Harry was her fellah
but only cos she said so.

Too scared to refuse,
he walked her home;

promised to sit with her
at the Saturday game.

They met at half past,
walked with the crowd

to the grassy goal end,
bumping shoulders

just a little too often.
If he had to kiss her

it would be his first.
At half time he heard

her whisper low
he loves me / he loves me not.

Surprised, he leaned in,
then saw her bitten fingers

slowly pulling the legs
from a living spider.

Iggy McGovern

HYPERMETROPIA

Apocryphal, no doubt, the story of
the Dublin Tommy who had lost an eye
for King & Country during The Great War.
When invalided back home he refused
to leave the house until he was supplied
with a glass eye, but one that would pass muster.
The first he judged the iris was too large,
the next too small, another the wrong shade
of blue, and so on; it was many years
before he finally emerged to find
The Second City now in rebel hands
and all the garrison decamped; that eye
might also have gone back with this direction:
'Request adjustment of far-sight correction'.

Emily Holt

OUR RED EVENING

Part of every dream, the train, loud, lunatic,
lifts a din of rail and rim through Greystones, Bray.

The sea – a net – sways and wraps
the evening in mist. Faces frost the window.

One woman up the coast, another down.
Sunset, and skin pales, glows. Is sheer.

No blood on the hospital sheets –
all in her head – and you, bloodshot now

on the train. Gone Dún Laoghaire, still
Rathdrum, Arklow – the train marks each exile

with a sign. But exile – how it sleeps now
in your mother's bones. What you put inside

you can't take back. So bí i do thost, child.
Let the silhouette of south hill on sea take you back

to water. Here, take a glass. Take a cup. Drink
your mother back. Drink your town back,

that town of men bent on hill-walking, wrist
-clawing, senseless straying. Gone, you

knew it still lived in your bone. Your own
daughter waits in the city. One woman,

another. The line of you will stretch –
You will walk together down the coast –

whether beside or into the water, hair down,
you will walk in white shifts your mothers made.

Dáibhidh Thomáis Albanach

SUPER-CELTS

Séamus Barra Ó Súilleabháin, *Beatha Dhónaill Dhuibh* (Cló Iar-Chonnacht, 2016), €10.
Simon Ó Faoláin, *Fé Sholas Luaineach* (Coiscéim, 2014), €7.50.
Diarmuid Johnson, *Rún na mBradán: Rogha Dánta Gaeilge 2005–2015* (Coiscéim, 2016), €8.

As a sea-divided Gael resident in the Pictish kingdom of Aberdeenshire, I naturally associate Domhnall Dubh with the claimant to the Lordship of the Isles, imprisoned for decades by the Duke of Argyll, who died in Drogheda in 1545. As it happens, Séamus Barra Ó Súilleabháin's debut collection is a portrait of a different Dónall Dubh entirely. In truth Dónall is many people, but in 'Ardaingeal is ea Dónall Dubh' he is a daimon, a Mr Hyde figure, a Tyler Durden (later, there will be a poem about *Fight Club*), an unshakeable shadow 'seasta liom romham os mo chionn / mar sciath dofheicthe idir mé / is daoine eile...' When Dónall whispers into the narrator's ear, as he does in 'An Galar Dubhach', one wonders whether we aren't in an Irish *Dream Songs*, with Dónall taking the role of the friend who calls him 'Mr Bones' – the taunter and tempter, the comic foil, the pantomime villain. Whoever he is, seldom since Kavanagh's Patrick Maguire can a poetic proxy have been licensed to cause more devilment.

By way of parsing the satire in *Beatha Dhónaill Dhuibh*, let me suggest a comparison with the famous *feis* scene in Myles na gCopaleen's *An Béal Bocht*, and its Gaeilgeoir who insists it is not enough for Irish-speakers to speak Irish, they must use it exclusively to talk about Irish. This has conventionally been read as a satire on navel-gazing cultural nationalism, but suppose it's the other way round: a satire on people who hear Irish being used and assume, out of fear and ignorance, it can only be for reasons of truculent nationalism. As poetic memoir, the exuberant comedy of *Beatha Dhónaill Dhuibh* lends itself to just such a double interpretation. With its titular allusion to Christian hagiography, the collection harvests a hatful of obligatory ordeals for any self-respecting Irish life-story. Priests, poverty, unemployment, emigration, substance abuse all feature in gory detail. But Ó Súilleabháin's collection makes for a strangely insouciant misery memoir. So exuberant and knowing is the writing that the reader begins to suspect the whole thing is a parody, a satire on reader expectations and the marriage of trauma and kitsch in the age of *Angela's Ashes*. This reading, if true, is not a denial of misery and trauma, but a reframing of them in terms of questions of form and representation. Like Geoffrey Hill's Offa, Dónall enters the contemporary world from a realm of myth, and leaves in his wake quasi-archaeological traces; in 'Baile Fearthainne' he has become 'Rí Dónall', an Amergin figure present in the elements, and dissolving into folklore ('ó ní / nach ionadh / a bhuachaill/ tá a Dónall féin/ ag gach aon chlann', as we read in 'Cistin i mBaile an Sceilg'). Emigration provides Ó Súilleabháin with a particularly rich vein of satire. The usual Irish view of Irish-America is that it has parked itself down a historical siding, clinging to the emigrant's gesture, brogue, and faggot of useless memories, in MacNeice's phrase. Here though, it is often Ireland that is unreal in comparison to exilic elsewhere, as in 'Clocha', where Dónall discusses a race-riot in Philadelphia with a policeman in 1834, or 'Ag Filleadh Abhaile', with its melancholy comparison of Ireland and the States.

Present-day concerns are certainly present though: congratulations to Ó Súilleabháin for writing the first Irish-language poems I've read on pornography, jihadi videos, and transgender sex work. A poem about Gaoth Dobhair describes a cabaret, and I wondered whether this remarkable book is best understood as an explosion of that Bakhtinian stand-by, the carnivalesque, like the Cyclops chapter of *Ulysses* or the graveyard mutterings of *Cré na Cille*. As the collection draws to a close, it makes its peace (of a kind) with more conventional lyric utterance, as in the haiku of 'Gunsaku Tuathail'. Just as Dónall is many people, this collection is several books, each as unsettling as the next. Ó Súilleabháin seems to me a major new talent.

'Triallfam amárach ar inné arís', Simon Ó Faoláin wrote in a poem from his second collection, *As Gaineamh*: 'tomorrow we will embark again for yesterday'. Ó Faoláin is an archaeologist by trade, and knows all about living between present and past. In 'Réamhdhréacht', the first poem in the sequence 'Baile do Bhí', he sketches what threatens to be a generic Irish vista of a ruined cottage. Rather than rush in and perform a seasoned riff on themes of dispossession, the poet hangs back: 'Tugaimis sciuird / Thart ar imeall, / B'fhearr an cheist / A sheachaint tamall.' (There is a whole poem later on devoted to thresholds, a locale with evident appeal for Ó Faoláin). Further on in the sequence, in 'Snaidhm', he inverts the logic of poetic archaeology familiar from Heaney's *North*, whereby we reach back from the present to connect with the distant past. Initially he is rooting around in the wet earth on a mountainside, without feeling any living pulse in the relics he unearths. When he thinks of the pools of his childhood, however, he enters a world 'Atá chomh domhain / Le duibheagán', as deep as a chasm, and the Proustian unlocking of memory is underway.

'Frithlaoch' is an anti-heroic soliloquy, an off-key riposte to bardic *credos* such as Máirtín Ó Direáin's 'Cranna Foirtil'. Its speaker experiences the artistic life at an oblique angle to its usual outlets and platforms

('Gluaiseachtaí ní aithneoinn, / Sinn cleas na n-aonarán, / Ní bhailíonn Éigse Éireann / Le hais teas mo thinteáin'). The anti-heroic also finds its way into 'An Aois Nua' too, in which 'English Bob' and 'Mick the Monk' attempt to prognosticate winning lottery numbers from crystals. Still in England, there is more than one more layer of transcultural comedy at work in the satirical portrait of a 'spéirbhean' in 'Sna *Home Counties*'. Completing our tour of these islands, there are Welsh poems too, and even a Scottish *'bò Ghaidhleach'*.

While *Fé Solas Luaineach* keeps busy with its travels, in 'Folúntas I' it turns from lightly-ironised cultural encounters to the deeper subsoil of reality: 'Ní turas meafarach é seo, ach turas nithiúil anso ar domhan'. The landscape that follows here, and in 'Folúntas II', is drawn as though inexorably towards exposure and depopulation, but (as in 'Réamhdhreacht') in ways that reflect this collection's wariness of roots and fixed identity. When the poet attempts a self-portrait while looking out a window, in 'Scáil-Mhachnamh', the poem descends into a hall of mirrors of self and other, settling finally for the provisional truth of the in-between ('Sa spás idir ghloine phortráid is gloine na fuinneoige / Tá an tarna sciar de ré na bhfear mar shíoraíocht sínte'). To quote MacNeice again, this time his 'Train to Dublin': 'half-thought thoughts divide in sifted wisps.'

Fé Sholas Luaineach ends with an impressive bouquet of translations, from Anglo-Saxon and Eurpirides' *Medea*, among other sources. These are often introspective but engaged and impressive poems, field reports from the cliff edges of Ithaca and West Kerry. I have mentioned Ó Direáin's 'Cranna Foirtil', that robust *ars poetica*, and in 'Gallaras' (an elegy for Seamus Heaney), Ó Faoláin achieves a comparably impressive terseness and resolve: 'Seo mo ghuí, / Mian críonnacht'; / Deonaigh dom' / Dhán simplíocht.'

It comes as a surprise to open Diarmuid Johnson's *Rún na mBradán* and find it dedicated to me. Indirectly at least: having composed these poems in Germany, Romania, Brittany, and other parts, Johnson is moved to dedicate them to all 'do na Gaeilgeoirí atá ina gcónaí ar fud an domhain', i.e. those aforementioned sea-divided Gaels. A visit to Uist finds Johnson in elegiac mood. The sight of Clearance-era cottages brings down a pall of historical memory, with only here and there an elegant swan on the move: 'Ní amhlaidh an eala féin: / Ciúin gach loch dá slíocann sise / Leanann an tost í go humhal.' In 'Tús agus Deireadh' he finds ends in beginnings but also beginnings in ends, in an elegantly circular poem. Its way of looking at a blackbird rates an honorary number fourteen alongside the thirteen enumerated by Wallace Stevens:

> Tús sláinte díon
> Deireadh sláinte díbirt.

Tús áil ubh
Deireadh áil éigean.

Tús ceoil lon
Deireadh ceoil eala.

Incantatory anaphora is a recurrent habit (cf., 'Fear Siúil' and 'Dhíol mé mo Bhó'), often with an element of circling a place of origin or mysterious power. Johnson is one of those enviable super-Celts who bridge the P-Q language divide; born in Cardiff and raised in Ireland, he has also published poetry in Welsh. These poems cross centuries and cultures with the breeziness of Frank O'Hara jaywalking, as witness an address to Colmcille on Iona in 'Paidir Chásca', while the beautifully-sketched Scottish landscape of 'An Chéad Agallamh in Albain' might be an extract from *Agallamh na Seanórach* (Finn McCool on his summer holidays) or a spot of contemporary island-hopping.

All this is a roundabout way of suggesting that Johnson is classical in temperament, Celtic-Christian in his frame of reference, but not much use to a blurb-writer who fancied embroiling him in the dramas of post-Celtic Tiger Ireland. This book therefore leaves a slightly paradoxical impression. The fine poems of *Rún na mBradán* speak very recognisably from the Celtic world, but might not always strike the Anglophone reader (who, after all, will not read this book) as forming a very *Irish* book of poetry. When Johnson writes a poem about the border it is a rather than the border, and one that lacks the knowing political allegorising of the everyday that underlies so much Northern Irish poetry. Like the pit-horse in 'Capall Faoi Thalamh', his works seems to inhabit an invisible territory, closed to the usual Anglophone perspectives. In a strangely moving passage from Seán Ó Ríordáin's diaries quoted by Barry McCrea in his *Languages of the Night*, that great poet complains that Anglophone Irish poetry was '*ró-Éireannach*' in approach, 'too Irish' ('The fault I see with the English-language literary tradition in Ireland is that it is too centred on Ireland, always talking about Ireland ...'). He distrusted this, and felt his muse was calling him elsewhere. Imagine if readers could approach poetry in Irish not as a shortcut to some notional essence of Irishness, but (in this case) as a way of bypassing those debates altogether in favour of a poetry of clean lines, floating landscapes, and the slow-burn of that 'hard, gem-like flame' invoked by Walter Pater.

I read all three of these volumes with instruction and delight.

Jane Clarke

HE STOOD AT THE TOP OF THE STAIRS

insisting he could go down himself
but, like a frightened bullock refusing
the crush, his body wouldn't move

from the spot where I used to sit
in the dark listening to rows in the kitchen
when my mother showed him the bill

from the shop. He stood at the top
of the stairs in a fever that came on him
as fast as nightfall in winter,

steep, narrow steps between him
and the ambulance ticking
outside the back door.

He stook there in checked pyjamas
and thick Wellington socks,
in the house where he was born

and had sworn he would never leave.
I held him from behind,
my brother in front

coaxing with a tenderness
I'd never seen between them,
come on Dad, just one step, one step.

Tom French

BANK

There was a rhythm to the cut and catch.
        He cut. You looked. He swung. It flew. You caught.
He cut. You looked. He swung. It flew. You caught –
        a form of talk that obviated talk.

Work made all speech useless, so the silence
        passed between us and entered into us
and became, with each spit, one spit deeper,
        a ghost bank growing on the spreading ground.

When it came to it in the funeral parlour,
        unsure as yet our job of work was done,
I could not keep my two eyes off of him,

and kept, from habit, a *sleán*'s length from him,
        not to be caught on the end of his swing,
in case he had one last good swing in him.

Stephen Sexton

THE CURFEW

The radicals sprung the locks that night, hurrah!
and their lovely collarbones were almost moonly.

Rhinos shrieked and bellowed, elephants tromboned
and the animals nosed into town.

Sunrise to sunrise and sunrise we kept indoors.
If you can't count your onions, what can you count

my grandfather used to say. He said a lot of things.
Among the other miners he was legendary:

when no more than the thought of the pink crumple
of his infant daughter's body came to mind

a glow would swell in the pit, the men
would mayhem bauxite by the light

his tenderness emitted.
Some of me lived inside her even then.

The memorial fountain says nothing
of the weeks before the rescue failed

but mentions God which, as my grandfather
used to say, is just the name of the plateau

you view the consequences of your living from.
Or something like that. He said a lot of things.

He grew wise and weary as an albatross
and left for that great kingdom of nevertheless.

It would have pleased his handsome shoulders
to watch this Grizzly scoop for salmon

in the fountain of his friends, or the Bengals,
or the shakedown squad of chimpanzees

who bang and bang on the grocery window.
One by one eleven miners starved to death.

In the streets they collar or tranquillise
the ocelots and run a spike of ketamine

through the plumbing in the fountain.
Dromedaries blue-mood around the pub

aloof under their reservoirs of fat.
I don't sleep, but oh plateau! these days

of violence have been my happiest.
Even a cabbage is not without desire

my grandfather said one day, and now
among the animals, I feel under my wings

the words for things I thought I knew
departing, and I understand him.

'The Curfew' is the winner of the Poetry Society's 39th National Poetry Competition, announced in London on 29 March 2017

Ron Houchin

ROY ORBISON'S GLASSES

To me, they are, more than Beethoven's hair or Einstein's brain,
possibility, more important than authenticity or the truth.

Found in a Vernon, Texas pawnshop, atop a leather glasses case
inscribed with gold R.K.O. – said my friend who sent them.

He kept the case, mailed me the spectacles. I know they are unlikely
the Big O's, any more than red words are actually Jesus's in the Bible,

but they have leeway. Thick, smoky magnifiers in black frames.
Not sure I want them to be real. Not just a faith that there are

things out there worth twenty-four dollars and fifty cents, glasses
no one else will ever wear, but that we think there are. They lie

on the shelf of my vinyl collection, a lie, like most things sacred.
Reality radiates a little thicker around them, like air around the chopped off

saint's finger, the gouged-out eye that's seen too much, a deer skull hung
on a fence – horns and all – rotting into the next six seasons. These lenses

won't be destroyed. They have power, *Mystery Girl* before the heart
attack, a lottery ticket, frail paper, retaining power until the drawing.

Joseph Woods

LET US FLY AWAY TO THE FAMED CITIES OF ASIA

ad claras asiae volemus urbes
             – Catullus 46

A mini Manhattan of rusted corrugated roofs
settling in to the sixth storey of a recently
red raw apartment. No longer the sole occupants
of the building which was eerie in evenings
despite days – seven days a week – of building site
aural accompaniment. That too is dying down,
in so far as noise in this neck of the woods
ever dies down. We live with drills and the thuds
of lump-hammers on ceilings, we breakfast
to angle-grinders slicing in the landing
of a Sunday morning while everything
is being built, dismantled and demolished
by hand and carted out in bamboo baskets
on people's heads through long corridors of dust.

No one ever complains, it's part of the old city
disappearing and the new one rising, refashioning
in front of our eyes to the ambient and atonal
music of construction. Our kitchen faces east
and each evening a clockwork sun drops
with southern hemisphere promptness
behind sprouting new high-rises on the horizon
breaking the sun's fall by seconds.
Home, a citadel of sorts with 180-degree views
of the neighbourhood; high-density living on one side
and on the other, an auspicious view of the golden stupa
of the Shewdagon, whose bricks, under its thickening
skin of gold, were laid; one layer by men by day
and one layer by celestials at night.

Across the narrow canyon, cross-sections of lives
and where it not for street noise and language
we could almost lean out and converse.
Sometimes, a house phone rings
in the evening, so audible,
it could be in our own apartment.
I see someone move to answer it and later
the unfurling of bedrolls on polished parquet
floors which in this high heat, incenses rooms
with the tang of teak. Our two-year-old daughter
abed and under a muslin dome for mosquitoes,
asks that her bedtime story, 'has a garden in it'
and later, 'where's home', as I direct the fan
to her soon sleeping form.

She loves the gekko who moved in ahead of us,
clicking loudly at night like a wren in a hedge
at home and we are glad of its industry. Evenings
fill with new noises, honking geese in an alleyway
below, kept to keep snakes away. Demonic
crows gathering on the gigantic and shedding cotton
tree at dusk and then seasonally, choruses of frogs
grunting then squawking like birds and cicadas
whose shrill rises to our level at the point
you can hardly hear yourself. Nights of wakefulness,
drawn from bed to the drone of a monk reciting sutras
through a tannoy all night, and peering through the kitchen
window to find another, golden pagoda, many miles
away, ethereally illumed by a roseate half-moon.

Distant pariah dogs howling, gathering into packs
to roam through compliant streets. The night train's
dying concertina note to Mawlamyine or Mandalay
and times when I've lain awake, waiting
for the affirmation or release of the soft-gong
of our nearest monastery at 4.30 a.m. or the downtown
mosque's muffled call to prayer. Once, called to the kitchen
to find the room throbbing with the hum of boat engines
on the Yangon river, a sound that only occasionally
reached us having travelled through the empty boulevards,
at dawn, before the early caterwauls of street sellers
and breakfasts arriving on the backs of bikes,
from boiled pulses to parathas delivered to your door
or sometimes attached to a coloured nylon cord.

Coloured cords which dangle from every balcony
primed with a crocodile clip on one end
or a basket in which to haul up the matter
of the whole world; newspapers, mangoes,
laundry and lottery tickets like pinned butterflies
go up while money and letters are lowered down.
And if all else fails, simply step out and clap,
someone will brave the steep stairs and appear
at your door as if by magic. Already the heat is up,
not that it dropped much during the night,
and leaving the air-conditioned citadel
is to dip your toe into the cauldron and chaos.
Heat entraps and like Shelley's worm, dissipates
and dissuades you from setting out.

All day scrutiny of the sun, someday we'll exchange
this heat for the cold, wind and rain,
our daughter pines for and wish it all back again,
disillusioned by the eternally false promises of our own.
Right now, a monotony of washed blue skies and water
in the cold tap that can scald by noon.
At street level, a woman walks ahead with a tin basin balanced
on her head, fish tails and chicken feet, imploring the sky
with some fish and fowl riddle.
Late afternoon, noise abated, my daughter calls me
to the living room and the faint tinkling of a bell
which neither of us can find. Too soft for the monastery,
then overhead, glass lozenges in the garish Chinese chandelier
shake and make music to the latest earth tremor.

Martin Malone

TROUBADOURS

Simon Armitage, *The Unaccompanied* (Faber and Faber, 2017), £14.99.
Peter Sirr, *Sway* (The Gallery Press, 2017), €11.95.

One is reluctant to characterize the work of a poet who's proved himself to be as versatile as Simon Armitage in the past few years, nevertheless, it is difficult to disagree with the accompanying press release when it describes this collection as 'a return to his trademark contemporary lyricism'. Following those hugely enjoyable shaggy dog stories of 2010's *Seeing Stars*, and recent forays into literary translations of everything from the classics to medieval alliterative poetry, *The Unaccompanied* returns to territory, perhaps, more familiar to fans of his earlier work: the finely tuned, multi-textured and darkly humorous lyric. With a writer who came to prominence at such a precociously early age and who is now publishing his eleventh major poetry collection, I suppose, too, that issues of canonicity bleed through into our response: we are, God willing, looking at prime mid-period Armitage; at a collection commensurate with, say, *Electric Light* or *District and Circle*. The Heaney connection is not altogether irrelevant here because, although very different poets, each manage consistently to pull off that intangible trick of stars which poetry can do in the hands of a master craftsman in full possession of his or her material. The last time I was so profoundly impressed by a collection's ingrained accomplishment was when reading *Human Chain*. Let's not beat about the bush, then, *The Unaccompanied* is something of a *tour de force*.

Armitage has always been a master of just riding the wince of his lines, lines which frequently host imagery that drags everyday subject matter into much darker territory. It's what has drawn comparisons to Larkin and is here evident from the start: 'The Last Snowman' obliquely chronicles our melting ice caps whilst sporting a clay pipe which 'drooped from a mouth / that was pure stroke victim'. And the opening sequence of poems show-cases this sure-footed regard of a world in slowly accelerating change beyond old certainties and givens. The ragged sonnet of 'Nurse at a Bus Stop' is as poised and finely-judged a social comment as anything around right now, deftly sketching this 'Jilted bride of public transport', stood waiting to go perform her benevolent duties in a winter world where 'The centuries crawl past, / none of them going your way'. In 'Emergency', 'Poundland' and 'The Empire', we see decline's last stop on its own spectrum before total loss; where social signifiers of 21st-century diminution – the skeleton workforce, up-for-rent fire station, makeshift crew of volunteer part-timers and wide boys in white socks – are employed as expertly as Pa Heaney's peat shovel. At times, *The Unaccompanied* is a lesson in the powers of artful and restrained social comment pegged confidently to the poet's craft, a craft that is never overpowered by the importance of its message. Indeed, in a world of hair-trigger online hysteria, Armitage provides us with a timely reminder that, if message there be, this is how to bring it home.

Which is not to say that *The Unaccompanied* is exclusively a well-turned but furrow-browed state-of-the-nation address. Armitage has a canny way with the interior dynamics of a poetry collection, altering the pace and flow of this one with flurries of linked poems, such as the two still-lives of 'A Bed' and 'A Chair', or the Dad n' Lad sequence of 'Privet', 'Prometheus', and 'Harmonium'. These serve to keep the reader alert and attuned to the ebb-and-flow of the poems, and the rhythms of the book as a whole. There is, too, a liberal sprinkling of the mock-heroic – to which Armitage has never been averse – in poem's like 'Maundy Thursday', 'The Keiran', and 'Deor', which echoes his recent translation work with its archaisms and *faux* alliterative style. We even get a villanelle about the serial killer Robert Maudsley, that reclaims the form, somewhat, for the modern world (though, as we shall see, Peter Sirr might point out its proto-punk moment long before now). Beyond the quiet lyricism, humour and elegant chutzpah familiar to longstanding fans, what *The Unaccompanied* reminds us of is the sheer quality of Simon Armitage's discrimination, and his unerringly good eye when it comes to matching moment with image. Many of these poems are also possessed of that apparent simplicity which only comes with writers at the top of their game. The late brace of poems about ageing embody these virtues beautifully. 'Old Boy' represents an almost Martian poetry of obsolescence in a century of ageing populations:

> A dancing bear from a flooded valley in the foothills I am relocated
> to the city of This Morning and cruelly set free.

This seemingly throwaway metaphor covers so much ground true to the world we inhabit, likewise the 'Saxon king unearthed in a ditch' of 'Poor Old Soul', whose carer throws back the curtain as:

> morning
> bursts like a water balloon before he can rig up
> his tatty umbrella of epidermis and bone.

Impossible to do justice to such a collection in the limited space of a review, one can only recommend *The Unaccompanied* to readers and writers with a genuine regard for the enduring possibilities of the contemporary lyric.

Not so much a return to form, then, as a reminder of that more permanent thing: class.

Longstanding personal connections to the Languedoc meant that I approached Peter Sirr's new collection with some degree of enthusiasm. I was not disappointed. His 'Versions of Poems from the Troubadour Tradition' plays fast and loose with elements of the originals whilst retaining their spirit in an attempt 'to find a matching music in English'. This has to have been a good decision, since Sirr has also managed to reinvigorate his material with the patina of contemporaneity in a dynamic rendition of twelfth- and thirteenth-century skull candy. Ezra Pound's rediscovery of Troubadour poetry sits well with Sirr's claims for its origination of European lyric poetry as we know it, but, in practice, there is something altogether more skittish and enjoyable abroad here, closer to Nick Cave than Modernist experiment. Nowhere is this more evident than in those pieces celebrated in Sirr's Afterword as 'meta-poems', which play comfortably with the idea of poetry in a manner entirely familiar to the twenty-first century reader: poems like Bernart de Ventadorn's 'Time comes and goes ...' or Arnaut Daniel's 'When the leaf falls ...' Here the lorn lover's hopes for his song to 'do your thing' put me in mind of nothing so much as Cave's 'Love letter Love Letter / Go get her Go get her'. And Sirr's greatest achievement here is the general spirit of song and freestyling which pervades this collection, literally allowing it to take 'flyte' in places. Not that all this precludes some impressive translation work from Old Occitan, nor success in retaining that original spirit of the Troubadour flowering in the latter part of the twelfth century. There is, too, some deft handling of its matching music in twenty-first century English, apparent also in Sirr's original poems inspired by the tradition, such as the book's 'Coda', or 'Lines for the poet Macabru', who 'shivers in the meadow / ice on his tongue, bitter his song'. Here, Sirr shows us the possibility for a form of re-tooled, re-energised poetry inspired by the Troubadour tradition, though not so sonorous and self-consciously archaic as Pound's translations, more trimmed to contemporary registers.

Like John Le Mesurier, the Troubadour poets suffer beautifully, their courtly tradition demanding its riffs on unrequited love and performative fortitude on the part of the spurned suitor, 'who can't help loving her / from whom I'll have nothing'. There is an interesting distinction between this trope and that which characterizes the few female voices here present, such as Clara d'Anduza and Beatriz de Dia. Where the men gild their existential plight with big abstractions, these women tend to lament an actual physical separation, which makes their verses both more poignant and somehow more carnal. Perhaps what I like most about this collection, however, is its vibrant translation of the dominant rhythms of Troubadour poetry: the natural world and seasons turning in an age unencumbered by quite so much trivial materiality. The book is alive with birdsong and trees shedding or coming into leaf, as lovers find natural correlatives to their own rising sap, or as Benart de Ventadorn has it:

> When the woods and the hedgerows
> put on leaves and the flowers
> come out and spring greens gardens
> and meadows again and the
> mournful birds cheer up, likewise
> I too find my voice and my
> greened spirit comes into leaf.

In moments like these the influence of Troubadour poetry upon the later English music of Chaucer becomes most apparent, and Sirr succeeds in illuminating his case for them to be regarded as the founders of much that came after. His achievement in doing so is considerable, never less than entertaining and their 'torch flaring / down the centuries / to where it all began' is re-ignited in some style.

Shirley Gorby

VISITING THE SEAMSTRESS

The bulb's flash calls her to the door.
She cannot hear or speak, but smiles
leading mother and I down the hall
to a room that smells of cloth
sewn with threads of smoke,
where the sewing machine faces a wall.

On a table by the window, a cup of biros,
a stack of paper – unlined square sheets
like baking parchment, yet lighter.
Their writing hands –
mouths with voices of ink;
gossip flows onto empty sheets.

In laughter, the shrill sound
of my mother intrudes,
and so I choose
not to hear, but watch
two faces, two bodies uncontrollably move
toward each other and back.

I read used pages,
and crumpling the names of neighbours
and mothers of school friends
into the bad happenings penned,
my hands become feet
trampling leaves to a whisper.

On leaving the silence of that house,
a wastepaper basket brims
with an afternoon's conversation,
bar one sheet of paper that lies
hidden in a child's coat pocket;
so deftly folded onto itself,
it can no longer breathe.

Conor Cleary

WEBBING
   – for Toby

what would you say
if it turned out
I was a giant
mechanical
spider who
didn't really
like the things we
both said we liked

if on further
inspection you
were to discover
my insides are
chock-full of
counterfeit silk
and I hated
your friend Rachel

what if my gums
concealed big steel
fangs needed to eat
that retracted
seamlessly
that envenomed
that were very
much part of me

I hope that you'd
take a step back
think rationally
try to see things
as seen from
my perspective
hung upside down
from the ceiling

Majella Kelly

MICHAELMAS DAISIES

The fishing has finished. It is the beginning
of hunting season. It is the time to pick apples
and the time to make cider.

A lost flock of Sebastopol geese
shuffle from a pond on Stephen's Green.
They do not know that it is Michaelmas.

Their eyes are ocean blue, their down
a flounce of soft white curls, matted
under filthy blankets and damp cardboard.

The streets are impractical
for their gaudy orange slippers. When handled
carefully, they are chatty and gregarious

but when ruffled, can be haughty and raucous.
Some gorge on blackberry cider,
sickly-sweet as if the devil himself had pissed in it.

Others place stones on their tongues,
to muffle their honking, so they can peck
undetected in the bins outside McDonald's.

More settle in Georgian doorways,
beak under wing, with scribbled petitions
hung from their gizzards.

These geese now bedizen the city, perennially,
like the blue and purple hues of Michaelmas daisies
that grow in wayside places, with no care at all.

Notes on Contributors

Dáibhidh Thomáis Albanach has contributed translations from the Irish to *The Penguin Book of Irish Poetry* (Penguin Books, 2010), and Louis de Paor's *Leabhar na hAthghabhála/Poems of Repossession* (Bloodaxe Books / Cló Iar-Chonnacht, 2016). He is currently learning Scots Gaelic.

Jean Bleakney lives in Belfast. Her *Selected Poems* was published in 2016, and a new collection is forthcoming, also from Templar Poetry.

Kevin Cantwell has published two books of poems, the most recent of which is *One of Those Russian Novels* (2009). His work has appeared in *Poetry, Irish Pages, Commonweal, The Paris Review*, and *The New Republic*. A group of his poems was published in *Five Points* as winner of the James Dickey Poetry Prize. He is Professor of English and Dean of Graduate Studies at Middle Georgia State University (USA).

Liam Carson is the director of the IMRAM Irish Language Literature Festival, and the author of the memoir *call mother a lonely field* (Hag's Head Press/Seren Books, 2012).

Jane Clarke's first collection, *The River*, was published by Bloodaxe Books in 2015. In 2016 she won the inaugural Listowel Writers' Week Poem of the Year Award and the Hennessy Literary Award for Emerging Poetry, and *The River* was shortlisted for the Royal Society of Literature Ondaatje Prize.

Conor Cleary is from Tralee, Co Kerry and lives in Belfast. He is currently studying poetry at Queen's University, where he was the recipient of this year's Seamus Heaney Centre MA Award. He is a participant in this year's Poetry Ireland Introduction Series.

Colette Colfer is originally from Hook Head in Co Wexford. She now lives in Waterford City where she lectures part-time in world religions at Waterford Institute of Technology. She previously worked as a journalist and is an award-winning radio documentary maker.

A.M. Cousins' poetry has appeared in *The Best New British and Irish Poets 2017* (Eyewear Publishing), *The Stinging Fly, The SHop, The Honest Ulsterman, The Irish Literary Review*, and *Skylight 47*. Her work was highly commended in The Patrick Kavanagh Poetry Competition in 2015 and 2016; and she featured in Poetry Ireland's Introductions Readings in 2016.

Susannah Dickey is a final year student of English with Creative Writing at Queen's University, Belfast. Her poetry has been published in *Ambit*, *The Tangerine*, and the anthology *The Best New British and Irish Poets 2017* (Eyewear Publishing). She was the winner of the inaugural Verve Poetry Competition, and is a participant in this year's Poetry Ireland Introductions Series.

Katie Donovan has published five collections, all with Bloodaxe Books. Her most recent, *Off Duty*, was shortlisted for the 2017 *Irish Times* Poetry Now Award, and she is this year's recipient of the Lawrence O'Shaughnessy Award for Irish Poetry. She teaches Creative Writing at NUI, Maynooth.

Theo Dorgan's most recent publications are *Nine Bright Shiners* (The Dedalus Press, 2014), the recipient of the 2015 *Irish Times* Poetry Now Award, and two volumes of translation from the French of Syrian poet Maram al-Masri: *Barefoot Souls* (2015) and *Liberty Walks Naked* (2017), both with Arc Publications. He is a member of Aosdána.

Kenneth Fields studied poetry with Edgar Bowers at UC Santa Barbara and with Yvor Winters at Stanford University, where he has been teaching for fifty quick years. His most recent book of poems is *Classic Rough News* (Phoenix Poets, 2005). He is collecting a book of essays, *On the Loose*, and a new and selected poems, *The Hunter Deep in Summer*. He is also writing an essay on Richard Wilbur and Edgar Bowers.

Leontia Flynn's most recent collection is *Profit and Loss* (Cape Poetry, 2011). She won the AWB Vincent American Ireland Fund Literary Award in 2014.

Tom French's work is published by The Gallery Press. He is currently editing *A Bittern Cry*, an anthology of writing on Francis Ledwidge in the centenary year of his death.

Shirley Gorby lives in Dublin. Her poems appeared in *The Irish Times* as part of the Hennessy New Irish Writing series in March 2017. She is working on her first collection.

Richard W Halperin's most recent collection with Salmon Poetry is *Quiet in a Quiet House* (2016). A new collection, *Catch Me While You Have the Light*, is listed for Autumn, 2017. His most recent chapbooks for Lapwing are *Prisms* and *The House with the Stone Lions*.

Eithne Hand is a writer, producer, and curator from Greystones, Co Wicklow. She has published poetry in *THE SHOp*, *Southword*, *Crannóg*, and *The Irish Times*. Her work has been shortlisted for the Patrick Kavanagh Award, and was highly commended in the Gregory O'Donoghue Prize in 2016. She is working towards a first collection.

Michael Hofmann is a poet and essayist. His newest translation is of Franz Kafka's *The Burrow* (Penguin Books, 2017).

Wendy Holborow, born in South Wales, lived in Greece for 14 years, where she edited *Poetry Greece*. Her poetry has been published internationally and placed in competitions. She recently gained a distinction for a Masters in Creative Writing at Swansea University. Her collection *After the Silent Phone Call* was published by Poetry Salzburg in 2015; *An Italian Afternoon* is forthcoming from Indigo Dreams.

Emily Holt's essays and poems have appeared in *Brief Encounters: A Collection of Contemporary Nonfiction* (WW Norton and Co., 2015), *The Honest Ulsterman*, *Abridged*, and *Talking River*. She has worked as a journalist, editor and caregiver in the US and Ireland, and has taught poetry in youth jails and hospitals.

Ron Houchin is a retired public school teacher living on the banks of the Ohio River, across from his hometown of Huntington, West Virginia. His most recent book, *Planet of the Best Love Songs,* was released in February 2017, by Salmon Publishing. He has seven previous books of poetry and one book of short stories. His awards include the Weatherford Award for Poetry (2013).

Andrew Jamison was born in Co Down. His first collection, *Happy Hour*, was published in 2012. His second collection, *Stay*, also with The Gallery Press, will be published in September 2017.

Diarmuid Johnson was educated in Galway (MA, Ph.D.), and has been writing for thirty years. He is the author of two volumes of poetry in Irish, *Súil Saoir* (Cló Iar-Chonnacht, 2004), and *Rún na mBradán* (Coiscéim, 2016); two works of prose in Welsh, *Y Gwyddel* (Gomer, 2011) and *Tro ar Fyd (*Y Lolfa, 2013); and *Pen and Plough* (Carreg Gwalch, 2016), a study of the bardic tradition in West Wales. He is also an accomplished musician, and will be reading and playing in 2017 in Wales, Brittany, Germany, and Ireland.

Brigit Pegeen Kelly – see page 20.

Majella Kelly is from Tuam. Her work is published or forthcoming in the *Aesthetica Creative Writing Annual 2017*, *The Best New British and Irish Poets 2017* (Eyewear Publishing), *The Irish Times,* and elsewhere. She is currently doing the Master of Studies in Creative Writing at Oxford, and is a participant in this year's Poetry Ireland Introductions Series.

John Kinsella's most recent books include *Drowning in Wheat: Selected Poems* (Picador Poetry, 2016), and *A Shared Wonder of Light: Poems and Photographs from West Cork and Kerry* (with photographer John D'Alton). He is a Fellow of Churchill College, Cambridge University, and Professor of Literature and Sustainability at Curtin University, Western Australia.

Aifric Mac Aodha's first collection, *Gabháil Syrinx*, was published by An Sagart in 2010. She is a former editor of *Comhar*, and the current Irish-language poetry editor of *The Stinging Fly, Gorse,* and Poetry Ireland's *Trumpet*. The Arts Council of Ireland has awarded her several bursaries. She works as an assistant editor with An Gúm.

Thomas McCarthy is a former editor of *Poetry Ireland Review*. Born in Cappoquin, Co Waterford, he was educated at University College Cork. He worked for Cork City Libraries until 2014 when he left to write full-time. He has published two novels, two books of non-fiction and nine collections of poetry, including *The First Convention* (The Dolmen Press, 1978), *The Lost Province* (Anvil Press, 1996), *Merchant Prince* (Anvil Press, 2005) and *Pandemonium* (Carcanet Press, 2016). He is a member of Aosdána.

Iggy McGovern is Fellow Emeritus in Physics at Trinity College, Dublin. The Dedalus Press published two of his collections, *The King of Suburbia* (2005) and *Safe House* (2010). His most recent publication is *A Mystic Dream of 4* (Quaternia Press, 2013), a poetic biography of the 19th century Irish mathematician, William Rowan Hamilton.

Anne Maher is a member of the 'Mullingar Scribblers' writing group, and has published in their five anthologies. Her work is also included in *Boyne Berries, Riposte, Midland Arts Magazine, Loose Leaves, Out of the Shadows,* and *The Huffington Post*.

Martin Malone, born in Co Durham, now lives in Scotland. He has published two poetry collections – *The Waiting Hillside* (Templar Poetry, 2011), and *Cur* (Shoestring Press, 2015). His Great War-related third collection, *The Unreturning*, will be published in 2018. An Honorary Research Fellow in Creative Writing at Aberdeen University, he has just completed a Ph.D. in poetry at Sheffield University. He edits *The Interpreter's House*, a poetry journal.

Jean O'Brien's fifth and latest collection, *Fish on a Bicycle: New and Selected Poems*, was published by Salmon Poetry in 2016. She has won prizes in the Arvon International Award, The Fish Poetry Prize, and the Forward Prize, among others. She holds an M.Phil. in Creative Writing from Trinity College, Dublin and tutors in creative writing.

Proinsias Ó Drisceoil's books include *Ar Scaradh Gabhail: An Fhéiniúlacht in Cin Lae Amhlaoibh Uí Shúilleabháin* (Clóchomhar, 2000) and *Seán Ó Dálaigh: Éigse agus Iomarbhá* (Cork University Press, 2007). He is the author of many essays on cultural history and on the Gaelic poetry, literature and language of Ireland and Scotland, and on traditional song.

Michael O'Loughlin was born in Dublin. A graduate of Trinity College, Dublin, he is a poet, translator, screenwriter, and critic. His most recent publication is *Poems 1980-2015* (New Island Books, 2017). He is a member of Aosdána.

Paul Perry is the author of five critically-acclaimed collections of poetry, including *Gunpowder Valentine* (The Dedalus Press, 2014), and three best-selling co-authored Karen Perry novels published by Penguin, including *The Boy That Never Was*, and *Girl Unknown*, both of which have been optioned for screen. He teaches creative writing at UCD, where he directs the MFA course in Poetry.

Thomas Dillon Redshaw edited the journals *Éire-Ireland* (1974 – 1996), and *New Hibernia Review* (1996 – 2006). In 2004 he published *Well Dreams: Essays on John Montague* with Creighton University Press. He is the author of articles on Thomas Kinsella, John Montague, James Liddy, George Reavey, Brian Coffey, and John F Deane, as well as a suite of essays on Liam Miller's Dolmen Press. *Mortal* (Brighthorse Books, 2017), is his third collection of poems.

John W Sexton's fifth poetry collection, *The Offspring of the Moon*, was published by Salmon Poetry in 2013. His poem 'The Green Owl' was awarded the Listowel Poetry Prize 2007 for best single poem, and in that same year he was awarded a Patrick and Katherine Kavanagh Fellowship in Poetry.

Stephen Sexton lives in Belfast. Poems have appeared in *Granta*, *Poetry London*, and *Best British Poetry 2015*. His pamphlet, *Oils*, published by The Emma Press, was the Poetry Book Society's Winter Pamphlet Choice. He was the recipient of an ACES award from the Arts Council of Northern Ireland in 2016, and is the winner of The Poetry Society's National Poetry Competition 2017.

Solmaz Sharif is the recipient of a National Endowment for the Arts Fellowship, a Stegner Fellowship, and most recently, a Lannan Literary Fellowship. Her first collection of poems, *Look* (Graywolf Press, 2016), was a finalist for the 2016 National Book Award. She is currently a lecturer at Stanford University.

Gerard Smyth has published nine collections of poetry, including, *The Yellow River*, with artwork by Sean McSweeney (Solstice Arts Centre, 2017), and *A Song of Elsewhere* (The Dedalus Press, 2015). He is co-editor of *If Ever You Go: A Map of Dublin in Poetry and Song* (The Dedalus Press, 2014).

Matthew Sweeney's most recent collection, *Inquisition Lane* (2015), is published by Bloodaxe Books. A previous collection, *Horse Music* (Bloodaxe Books, 2013) won the inaugural Pigott Poetry Prize. In between, there were two pamphlets in 2014, *The Gomera Notebook* (Shoestring Press) and *Twentyone Men and a Ghost* (The Poetry Business). A new book, *My Life as a Painter*, is forthcoming in late 2018.

Colm Tóibín is Irene and Sidney B Silverman Professor of the Humanities at Columbia University. His most recent book is *House of Names* (Simon and Schuster, 2017), a novel.

Laura Webb was born in Birkenhead. In 2006 she won the Blackwell Publishing / *The Reader* magazine 'How to Write a Poem' competition. She has had poems published in *CAST: The Poetry Business Book of New Contemporary Poets*, *Magma*, *Poetry Wales*, *Stand*, *The Rialto*, among other outlets. She lives in London.

Chelsea Whitton is an American poet and essayist. Her poems appear or are forthcoming in various web and print publications, including *Cimarron Review*, *Bateau*, *Forklift Ohio*, *WomenArts Quarterly*, *Main Street Rag*, and *Stand*. Her first chapbook, *Bear Trap*, is forthcoming from Dancing Girl Press. She lives in Ridgewood, Queens, with her husband and cat.

David Wheatley is the editor of *The Wake Forest Series of Irish Poetry*, Vol. 4 (Wake Forest University Press, 2017). His poetry collection, *The President of Planet Earth*, is forthcoming from Carcanet.

Joseph Woods lived in Burma in the lead up to democratic elections there. His fourth collection, *The Rain in Burma*, is forthcoming.

Poetry Ireland Review Editors

John Jordan 1–8 — Spring 1981–Autumn 1983
Thomas McCarthy 9–12 — Winter 1983–Winter 1984
Conleth Ellis and Rita E Kelly 13 — Spring 1985
Terence Brown 14–17 — Autumn 1985–Autumn 1986
Ciaran Cosgrove 18–19 — Spring 1987
Dennis O'Driscoll 20–21 — Autumn 1987–Spring 1988
John Ennis and Rory Brennan 22–23 — Summer 1988
John Ennis 24–25 — Winter 1988–Spring 1989
Michael O'Siadhail 26–29 — Summer 1989–Summer 1990
Máire Mhac an tSaoi 30–33 — Autumn 1990–Winter 1991
Peter Denman 34–37 — Spring 1992–Winter 1992
Pat Boran 38 — Summer 1993
Seán Ó Cearnaigh 39 — Autumn 1993
Pat Boran 40–42 — Winter 1993–Summer 1994
Chris Agee 43–44 — Autumn–Winter 1994
Moya Cannon 45–48 — Spring 1995–Winter 1995
Liam Ó Muirthile 49 — Spring 1996
Michael Longley 50 — Summer 1996
Liam Ó Muirthile 51–52 — Autumn 1996–Spring 1997
Frank Ormsby 53–56 — Summer 1997–Spring 1998
Catherine Phil MacCarthy 57–60 — Summer 1998–Spring 1999
Mark Roper 61–64 — Summer 1999–Spring 2000
Biddy Jenkinson 65–68 — Summer 2000–Spring 2001
Maurice Harmon 69–72 — Summer 2001–Spring 2002
Michael Smith 73–75 — Summer 2002–Winter 2002
Eva Bourke 76 — Spring/Summer 2003
Peter Sirr 77–91 — Autumn 2003–October 2007
Eiléan Ní Chuilleanáin 92–95 — December 2007–October 2008
Caitríona O'Reilly 96–99 — December 2008–October 2009
Paul Muldoon 100 — March 2010
Caitríona O'Reilly 101–104 — July 2010–September 2011
John F Deane 105–112 — December 2011–April 2014
Vona Groarke 113–120 — September 2014–December 2016